beauty basics

HAIRDRESSING AND BEAUTY INDUSTRY AUTHORITY SERIES

HAIRDRESSING

Mahogany hairdressing: Steps to cutting, colouring and finishing hair
Martin Gannon and Richard Thompson

Mahogany hairdressing: Advanced looks   *Richard Thompson and Martin Gannon*

Essentials, Next Generation Toni & Guy: Step by step professional men's
hairdressing   *Guy Kremer and Jacki Wadeson*

The art of dressing long hair   *Guy Kremer and Jacki Wadeson*

Patrick Cameron: Dressing long hair   *Patrick Cameron and Jacki Wadeson*

Patrick Cameron: Dressing long hair book 2   *Patrick Cameron*

Bridal hair   *Pat Dixon and Jacki Wadeson*

Trevor Sorbie: Visions in hair   *Kris Sorbie and Jacki Wadeson*

The total look: The style guide for hair and make-up professional   *Ian Mistlin*

Art of hair colouring   *David Adams and Jacki Wadeson*

Begin hairdressing: The official guide to level 1   *Martin Green*

Hairdressing – the foundations: The official guide to level 2   *Leo Palladino*
(contribution Jane Farr)

Prefessional hairdressing: The official guide to level 3   *Martin Green, Lesley
Kimber and Leo Palladino*

Men's hairdressing: Traditional and modern barbering   *Maurice Lister*

African–Caribbean hairdressing   *Sandra Gittens*

Salon management   *Martin Green*

Extensions: The official guide to hair extensions   *Theresa Bullock*

A holistic guide to massage   *Tina Parsons*

BEAUTY THERAPY

Beauty therapy – the foundations: The official guide to level 2   *Lorraine
Nordmann*

Beauty Basics: The official guide to level 1   *Lorraine Nordmann*

Professional beauty therapy: The official guide to level 3   *Lorraine Nordmann*

Aromatherapy for the beauty therapist   *Valerie Ann Worwood*

Indian head massage   *Muriel Burnham-Airey and Adele O'Keefe*

A holistic guide to anatomy and physiology   *Tina Parsons*

The encyclopedia of nails   *Jacqui Jefford and Anne Swain*

Nail artistry   *Jacqui Jefford, Sue Marsh and Anne Swain*

The complete nail technician   *Marian Newman*

The world of skin care: A scientific companion   *John Gray*

Safety in the salon   *Elaine Almond*

A holistic guide to reflexology   *Tina Parsons*

Nutrition: A practical approach   *Suzanne Le Quesne*

beauty basics

THE OFFICIAL GUIDE TO LEVEL 1

LORRAINE NORDMANN

HABIA

THOMSON

Australia • Canada • Mexico • Singapore • Spain • United Kingdom • United States

Beauty Basics: The official guide to Level 1

Copyright © Thomson Learning 2005

The Thomson logo is a registered trademark used herein under licence.

For more information, contact Thomson Learning, High Holborn House, 50–51 Bedford Row, London, WC1R 4LR or visit us on the World Wide Web at: http://www.thomsonlearning.co.uk

British Library Cataloguing-in-Publication Data
A catalogue record for this book is available from the British Library

ISBN 1-86152-936-8

First edition published 2005 by Thomson Learning

Typeset by The Partnership Publishing Solutions Ltd   **www.the-pps.co.uk**

Printed in Great Britain by The Bath Press

contents

foreword

It is a pleasure for me to write this foreword for *Beauty Basics*, which completes the pioneering trilogy of beauty therapy texts by Lorraine Nordmann.

Written to accompany a significant and exciting change within the industry – the introduction of the Level 1 beauty therapy qualification – for me, there was no question of who would write this text for the HABIA and Thomson Learning partnership.

An inspirational educationalist and practitioner, Lorraine has an abundance of industry knowledge and experience. She radiates professional aura, a result of her enthusiasm and passion for developing original learning materials for beauty therapists of all levels.

As you start your qualification and begin your career in a world full of opportunities, take Lorraine Nordmann's dedication and motivation as inspiration that great success can be achieved.

Alan Goldsbro
Chief Executive Officer, HABIA

introduction

AN INTRODUCTION TO NVQS

National Vocational Qualifications (NVQs) are nationally recognised qualifications and have a common structure and design. They follow a similar format for all occupational and vocational sectors. The award of an NVQ/SVQ (Scottish Vocational Qualification) demonstrates that the person has the competence (i.e. sufficient skill and knowledge) to perform job roles/tasks effectively in his/her occupational area.

An NVQ at Level 1 covers mainly routine work activities. In beauty therapy these include preparing and maintaining the work area and assisting others in their work roles. Your actions are important and will ensure the smooth running of the salon activities, reduce risks to health and safety, and improve the quality of the service offered to clients.

Each NVQ/SVQ is structured the same way, and is made up of a number of units and elements:

- The term **unit** relates to a specific task or skill area of work. It is the smallest part of the award that can be accredited separately.
- The **element(s)** describes in further detail the skill and knowledge requirements for each unit.

An example from NVQ Level 1 Beauty Therapy is given below:

- The title of the unit is Unit BT2: Assist with facial treatments.
- The elements for the unit detail the practical skills and underpinning knowledge essential to assist with facial treatments. The elements that detail the unit components include:

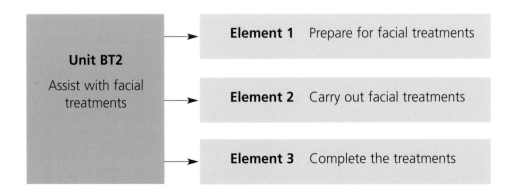

Units and elements

For each unit, when all competence requirements have been achieved, a unit of certification can be awarded, such as Unit BT2: Assist with Facial treatments.

Each NVQ is made up of a specific number of units required for the occupational area. For NVQ Level 1 Beauty Therapy, all the units are termed **mandatory units** (compulsory) and each must be competently achieved to gain the NVQ/SVQ award.

The following mandatory units make up the Beauty Therapy NVQ/SVQ qualification in **Beauty Therapy at Level 1** (all must be completed):

- G1: Ensure your own actions reduce risks to health and safety
- G2: Assist with salon reception duties
- BT1: Prepare and maintain the beauty therapy work area
- BT2: Assist with facial treatments
- BT3: Assist with nail treatments to the hands.

Performance criteria

The performance criteria list the necessary actions you must achieve to complete the task competently (demonstrating adequate practical skill and experience to the assessor). The **performance criteria** requirements for Unit BT2, Element 2: Carry out facial treatments (each stage of the facial treatment) are listed below:

a Maintain hygiene and safety throughout the treatment

b Using facial products correctly and following manufacturer's instructions

c Using suitable techniques to deep cleanse the client's skin

d Checking that the skin is left clean and free from all traces of make-up

e Applying pre-prepared non-setting mask treatments evenly and neatly, ensuring that the area to be treated is covered

f Removing masks after the recommended time and without discomfort to the client

g Applying the correct toner and moisturiser

h Ensuring that the skin is left clean, toned and suitably moisturised.

Range

Range statements are often identified for the different elements. The assessment range relates to the different conditions under which a skill must be demonstrated competently to pass the element. For example, the **range** assessment requirements for Unit BT2, Element 2 below lists the skin types to be covered:

Range Your performance must cover the following situations

Skin types are:
  a oily
  b dry
  c combination

It is not sufficient to be able to perform the task practically, you must **understand** why you are doing it and be able to transfer your competence to a variety of situations. This is called your **knowledge and understanding**. Further assessment of your knowledge and understanding of the skill, the knowledge specification, is made through theoretical tasks such as written tests, assignments and oral questioning.

The **knowledge and understanding** requirements required for **Unit BT2: Facial treatments** are listed below:

- the different cleansing techniques used within facial treatments and how to carry them out
- the reasons for cleansing, toning mask application and moisturising
- the benefits of cleansing, toning mask application and moisturising.

It is often the case that the same knowledge and understanding is necessary for similar units. This can be seen, for example, in the knowledge and understanding for **Organisational and Legal Requirements**.

Where evidence has been achieved this is cross-referenced (directed) in the portfolio (a file that holds your assessment evidence) in which the evidence can be found.

To achieve unit competence, all performance criteria, range and knowledge and understanding requirements must have been met and the necessary evidence presented. Evidence is usually provided in your assessment book and portfolio.

Beauty Basics – The Official Guide to Level 1 follows the Beauty Therapy NVQ/SVQ Level 1 format and covers both the practical and theoretical requirements for each mandatory unit. On successful completion of Level 1 Beauty Therapy you can progress and study towards an NVQ/SVQ Level 2 in Beauty Therapy.

You will then find all the practical and theoretical requirements for your new programme of study in *Beauty Therapy: The Foundations – The Official Guide to Level 2* (Thomson Learning, 2004).

BEAUTY BASICS – ABOUT THIS BOOK

The book relates to the NVQ/SVQ Level 1, 5-unit qualification structure and has five chapters each related to a specific NVQ/SVQ unit.

Features within chapters

Common features appear in the chapters, and an explanation of each is provided below:

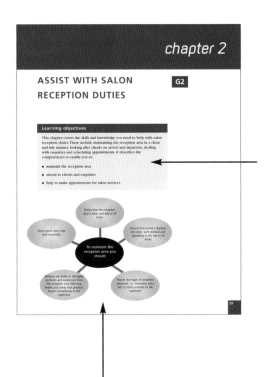

Learning objectives

All the chapters are introduced by the Learning objectives section, which lists the elements that make up the unit and which must be achieved in order to be accredited with the NVQ unit. When you feel confident and competent with the skills/knowledge requirements you are ready to be assessed.

Spidergrams

Spidergrams are provided in each chapter to summarise the skills/knowledge requirement for each element, with the title of the element in the centre of the spidergram. These provide a useful checklist.

Practical skills and knowledge checklist

The practical skills and knowledge checklist breaks down each stage of the treatment service. When you feel you have the necessary skills and knowledge in each area you can ask your assessor to assess you on the unit. These are provided for each unit.

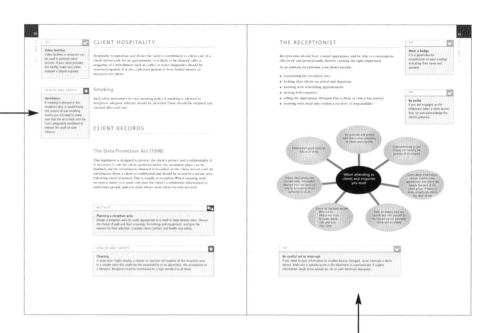

Health and safety boxes

In addition to Chapter 1 Unit G1: Ensure your own actions reduce risks to health and safety, health and safety boxes are provided in each chapter. They serve to draw your attention to related health and safety information for each technical skill.

Tip boxes

The author's experience is shared through tip boxes, which provide positive suggestions to improve your knowledge and skills for each unit.

Use of bold terms

The text highlights certain terms set in bold lettering, this information is often important or a technical term (explained in the glossary) that you must become familiar with to gain knowledge competence for the unit.

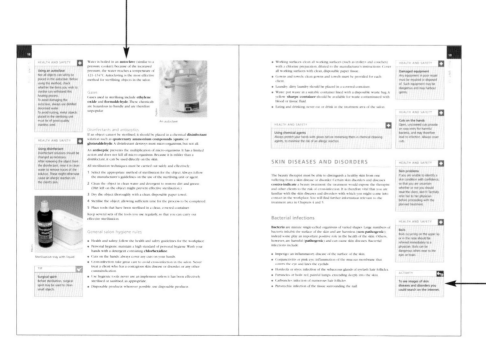

Activity boxes

Activity boxes feature within the chapters and provide additional tasks for you to complete to assess and further your understanding of the unit content.

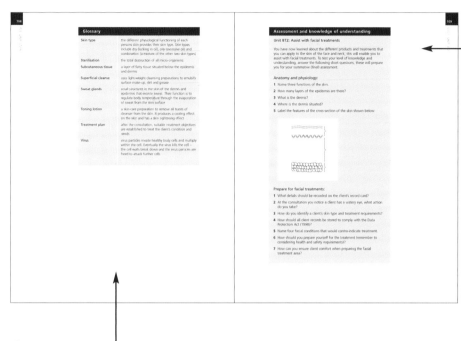

Glossary

A list of technical words, relevant legislation and their meanings is provided at the end of each chapter. This also provides a useful checklist to test your understanding.

Assessment of knowledge and understanding

In addition to the activity boxes in each chapter, questions are provided at the end of each chapter. These questions relate to the specific essential knowledge and understanding requirements for the unit. You can use the questions to prepare you for oral and written assessments. Seek guidance from your supervisor/assessor if there are any areas that you are unsure of.

Step-by-step photo sequences

Those chapters demonstrating a practical skill requirement contain step-by-step colour images to enhance your understanding.

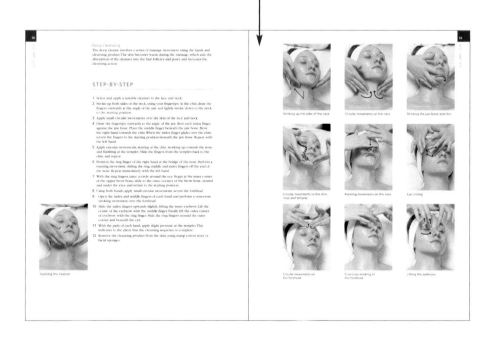

Treatment cards

Sample client treatment cards are featured. You are responsible for obtaining these before treatment and for storing them securely after treatment. These cards contain information that will be needed to establish client suitability and treatment aim; this information will be gained from the client at the consultation. The cards also record what information was provided after treatment, including aftercare advice and the promotion of additional products and services.

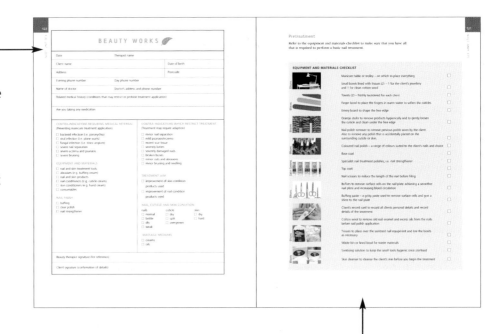

Equipment and material checklists

To help you prepare for each practical treatment, an essential equipment list is provided, supported with images of treatment tools, materials and products required. These are particularly useful when you are assisting to prepare the work area for Level 2 treatments.

Anatomy and physiology

Certain units have an anatomy and physiology knowledge requirement:

- BT2: Assist with facial treatments
- BT3: Assist with nail treatments.

The specific anatomy and physiology requirements for these units is discussed fully within the relevant chapters, without the need to refer elsewhere.

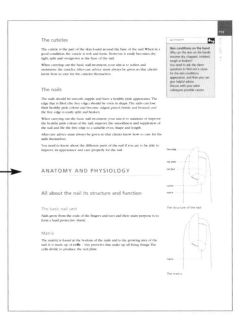

about the author

Lorraine Nordmann has over twenty years of experience in the beauty therapy industry – an industry she has seen grow significantly in status, technology and specialisms during her roles as lecturer, assessor and external verifier for City and Guilds. She aims to ensure that this high profile of the beauty therapy industry is maintained.

Lorraine is also the author of the HABIA official guides, *Beauty Basics* and *Beauty Therapy – the foundations*, covering the latest industry standards at NVQ/SQV levels 1 and 2.

acknowledgements

The authors and publishers would like to thank the following for their help
with providing images for the book:

Dr M. H. Beck
Adam Birtwistle at Sorisa
Diane Burkhill at Depilex
Chubb Fire Ltd
Dream Workwear
Dr John Gray
HMSO
Judith Iford
Emma Kenny and Pam Linforth at Ellisons
Sally Smith at Original Additions Ltd
Nicole Warwick at Designer Nails UK Ltd
Dr A. L. Wright

chapter 1

ENSURE YOUR OWN ACTIONS REDUCE RISKS TO HEALTH AND SAFETY

G1

Learning objectives

This chapter covers health and safety duties and responsibilities for everyone in the workplace. It describes the competencies required to ensure that:

- your own actions do not create any health and safety risks

- you do not ignore significant risks or hazards in your workplace

- you take sensible action to put things right, including reporting situations that pose a danger to people in the workplace and seeking advice where necessary.

Be aware of the workplace health and safety policy and your responsibility in its implementation

Ensure your working practice minimises the possible spread of infection or disease

Follow the workplace policies for your job role

To avoid potential hazards and risks in the workplace you should

Know the workplace fire evacuation and procedure

Follow the latest health and safety legislation related to your work

Be aware of first aid arrangements in the event of an accident or illness

Know who is responsible for health and safety in your workplace

Report immediately any risk which could be a hazard

PRACTICAL SKILLS AND KNOWLEDGE CHECKLIST

The table shown will help you to check your progress in gaining the necessary practical skills and knowledge for
Unit G1: Ensure your own actions reduce risks to health and safety.
Tick (✓), when you feel you have gained your practical skills and knowledge in the following areas:

	✓
1 The correct environmental conditions for each treatment, including: ● lighting ● heating ● ventilation ● general client comfort	
2 Preventing infection – selecting and using the correct method of sanitisation/sterilisation for tools, equipment and general salon hygiene	
3 Taking care of yourself, clients and colleagues following all health and safety requirements	
4 Wearing protective, hygienic clothing and maintaining a professional appearance	
5 Carrying out services in accordance with legal requirements and workplace policy	
6 Following the correct waste removal and disposal systems	
7 Knowing who to refer to for guidance on issues relating to health and safety in the workplace	
8 Avoiding potential hazards and risks within your job role, through safe working practices and personal conduct	
9 Knowing when to pass on information immediately, reporting potential risks or hazards to the relevant person	
10 Dealing with low-risk hazards within your responsibility, following workplace policy and legal requirements	
11 Following manufacturer's guidelines for the care and maintenance of equipment and product use and storage	
12 Knowing who to notify and the procedure to follow in the event of an accident or emergency	
13 Knowing the correct fire safety procedure to follow in the event of a fire	

HEALTH AND SAFETY

The Health and Safety Executive
The Health and Safety Executive (HSE) ensures that health and safety laws are being followed.
Two important aspects – hazards and risks – will be minimised if an effective workplace health and safety policy is followed:
Hazard: something with the potential to cause harm
Risk: the likelihood of a hazard's potential being realised.
It is important that hazards do not become risks.

When you have ticked all the areas you can ask your assessor to assess you on Unit G1: Ensure your own actions reduce risks to health and safety. After practical assessment, your assessor might decide that you need to practice further to improve your skills. If so, your assessor will tell you how and where you need to improve to gain competence.

INTRODUCTION

When working in the beauty therapy industry, you are legally obliged to provide a **safe and hygienic environment**. You must pay careful attention to health and safety practice to minimise risk.

HEALTH AND SAFETY IN THE WORKPLACE

Legal responsibilities

If you cause harm to your client, or put a client at risk, you will be held responsible and you will be liable to **prosecution**, with the possibility of being fined.

There is a good deal of **legislation** relating to health and safety. Details are widely available and you must be aware of your responsibilities and your rights. It is important that you obtain and read all relevant publications.

ACTIVITY

Keep updated
Health and safety information is continually being updated. Write to the Environmental Health Department of your local health authority department and ask for a pack of relevant health and safety information.

Legislation

The Health and Safety at Work Act (1974)

This Act developed from experience gained over 150 years and incorporates earlier legislation, including the Offices, Shops and Railway Premises Act (1963) and the Fire Precautions Act (1971). It lays down the minimum standards of health, safety and welfare required in each area of the workplace. For example, it requires business premises and equipment to be safe and in good repair. It is the employer's responsibility to implement the Act and to ensure that the workplace is safe both for employees and for clients.

All employers of more than five employees must have a written **health and safety policy** for that establishment. The policy must be issued to every employee and should outline their safety responsibilities. It should include items such as:

- details of the storage of chemical substances
- details of the stock cupboard or dispensary
- details and records of the checks made by a qualified electrician on specialist electrical equipment
- names and addresses of the person(s) with a key to the premises (the key holders)
- escape routes and emergency evacuation procedures
- rules on working practices

ACTIVITY

Health and safety rules
Discuss the rules which you feel should appear in a salon's health and safety policy.

HEALTH AND SAFETY

Health and safety notice
Every employer is obliged by law to display a health and safety notice in the workplace. This is required by the legislation Health and Safety (Information for Employees) Regulations 1989.

HEALTH AND SAFETY

Gloves
You should wear protective disposable surgical gloves if you are likely to come into contact with body tissue fluids or with chemicals.

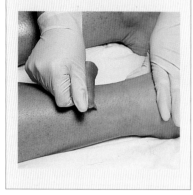

- personal presentation and hygiene
- rules on eating and drinking and drug use.

Regular checks should be made to ensure that safety is being satisfactorily maintained.

Employees must co-operate with their employer to provide a safe and healthy workplace. As soon as an employee observes a **hazard** this must be reported to the designated authority so that the problem can be put right. Hazards include:

- obstructions to corridors, stairways and fire exits
- spillages and breakages.

An obstruction occurs when an object blocks a traffic route or exit, creating a hazard. Obstructions are dangerous because they can cause accidents but also, in the event of an emergency such as a fire, an obstruction could prove fatal. Removing an obstruction is an example of avoiding potential hazard and risk in the workplace.

In 1992, European Union (EU) directives updated the legislation on health and safety management. Current legislation (at the time of writing – 2004) is outlined below.

ACTIVITY

Risk assessment
Carry out your own risk assessment. List the potentially hazardous substances handled in beauty therapy. What protective clothing should be available?

The Management of Health and Safety at Work Regulations (1999)

These require employers to make formal arrangements for maintaining and improving safe working conditions and practices. This includes training for employees and the monitoring of risk in the workplace, known as **risk assessment**.

The Personal Protective Equipment (PPE) at Work Regulations (1992)

These require managers to identify – through a **risk assessment** – activities or processes that require special protective clothing or equipment to be worn. This clothing and equipment must then be made available, in adequate supplies. Employees must wear the protective clothing and use the protective equipment provided, and should make employers aware of any shortage so that supplies can be maintained.

ACTIVITY

Health and safety: European directives
As a result of directives adopted in 1992 by the European Union, health and safety legislation has been updated. Obtain a copy of the new directives. Workplace (Health & Safety & Welfare) Regulations 1999.
Look through the publication, and make notes on any information relevant to you in the workplace.

The Workplace (Health, Safety and Welfare) Regulations (1992)

These require everyone at work to maintain a safe, healthy and secure working environment. The regulations include legal requirements in relation to the following aspects of the working environment:

- maintenance of the workplace and equipment
- ventilation
- working temperature
- lighting

- cleanliness and handling of waste materials
- safe salon layout
- falls and falling objects
- windows, doors, gates and walls
- safe floor and traffic routes
- escalators and moving walkways
- sanitary conveniences
- washing facilities
- drinking water
- facilities for changing clothing
- facilities for staff to rest and eat meals.

Manual Handling Operations Regulations (1992)

These regulations apply in all occupations that require manual lifting. The employer is required to carry out a risk assessment of all activities that involve manual lifting. The risk assessment should provide evidence that the following have been considered:

- risk of injury
- the manual movement involved in performing the activity
- the physical constraint the load incurs
- the environmental constraints imposed by the workplace
- workers' individual capabilities
- action taken to minimise potential risks.

Manual lifting and handling

Always take care of yourself when moving goods around the salon. Do not struggle or be impatient: get someone else to help. When **lifting**, lift from the knees, not the back. When **carrying**, balance weights evenly in both hands and carry the heaviest part nearest to your body.

TIP

Salon temperature
The salon temperature should be a minimum of 16°C within 1 hour of employees arriving for work. The salon should be well ventilated, or carbon dioxide levels will increase, which can cause nausea. Many substances used in the salon can become hazardous without adequate ventilation.
Lighting should be adequate to ensure that treatments can be carried out safely and competently, with the minimum risk of accident.

TIP

Unpacking
When you unpack a delivery, make sure the product packaging is undamaged.

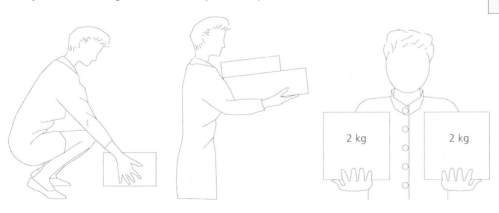

Left Lifting a box
Centre Carrying several boxes
Right Carrying equal weights in both hands

Provision and Use of Work Equipment Regulations (1998)

These regulations lay down the important health and safety controls on the provision and use of work equipment. They state the duties for employers and for users, including the self-employed. They affect both old and new equipment and identify the requirements for selecting suitable equipment and for maintaining it. They also discuss the information provided by equipment manufacturers, and the instruction and training in the safe use of equipment. Specific regulations address the dangers and potential risks of injury that could occur during operation of the equipment.

Health and Safety (Display Screen Equipment) (1992)

These regulations cover the use of visual display units (VDUs) and computer screens. They specify acceptable levels of radiation emissions from the screen and identify correct posture, seating position, permitted working heights and rest periods.

Control of Substances Hazardous to Health (COSHH) Regulations (1999)

These regulations were designed to make employers consider the substances used in their workplace and assess the possible risks to health. Many substances that seem quite harmless can prove to be hazardous if used or stored incorrectly.

Employers are responsible for assessing the risks from hazardous substances and controlling exposure to them to prevent ill health. Any hazardous substances identified must be formally recorded in writing and given a hazard risk rating. Safety procedures should then be implemented and employees trained to ensure that the procedures are understood and will be followed correctly.

Hazardous substances are identified by the use of symbols. Any substance in the workplace that is hazardous to health must be identified on the packaging and stored and handled correctly.

Hazardous substances can enter the body via the:

- eyes
- skin
- nose (inhalation)
- mouth (ingestion).

All beauty produce suppliers are legally required to produce guidelines on how materials should be used and stored. These are called material safety data sheets (MSDSs) and the manufacturer must supply these on request.

Electricity at Work Regulations (1989)

These regulations state that every piece of electrical equipment in the workplace must tested every 12 months by a qualified electrician. In addition to annual testing, a trained member of staff should check all electrical

ACTIVITY

COSHH assessment
Carry out a COSHH assessment on selected treatment products used in the salon. Consider manicures, nail treatments, waxing and facial and eye treatments.

COSHH
a brief guide to
the regulations

HSE

HMSO

equipment for safety; this should occur every three months. Report to your supervisor if you see any of these potential hazards:

- exposed wires in flexes
- cracked plugs or broken sockets
- worn cables
- overloaded sockets.

Although it is the employer's responsibility to ensure that all equipment is safe to use, it is also the responsibility of the employee to check that equipments is safe before use, and never to use faulty equipment.

Any pieces of equipment that appear faulty must be checked immediately and repaired (if faulty) before use. If faulty and unrepaired, they must be labelled so that they are not used by accident.

Accidents

Accidents in the workplace are usually the result of negligence by employees or unsafe working conditions. Any accidents occurring the workplace must be recorded on a **report form** and entered into an **accident book**. The report form requires more details than the accident book. You must note:

- the date and time of the accident
- the date of entry into the accident book
- the name of the person or people involved
- details of the accident
- the injuries sustained
- the action taken
- the signature of the person making the entry.

Hazard symbols

ACTIVITY

Identifying hazards
Make a list of potential electrical hazards in the workplace, e.g. damaged plugs. Who should these be reported to?

HEALTH AND SAFETY

Appoint a responsible person
It is useful to appoint a person to be responsible for maintaining the first aid equipment and for seeking assistance (if required) if there is not a designated first aider.

ACTIVITY

Avoiding accidents
Discuss potential causes of accidents in the workplace. How could these accidents be prevented?

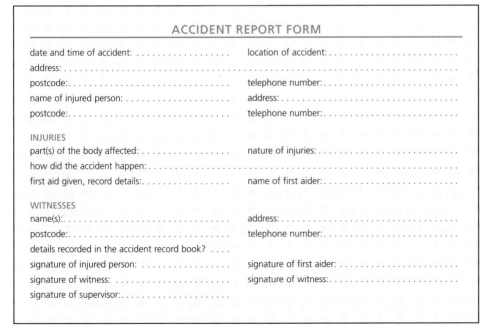

ACCIDENT REPORT FORM

date and time of accident: . . . .   location of accident:. . . . .
address: . . . .
postcode:. . . . .   telephone number:. . . . .
name of injured person: . . . .   address: . . . .
postcode:. . . . .   telephone number:. . . . .

INJURIES
part(s) of the body affected: . . . .   nature of injuries:. . . . .
how did the accident happen:. . . . .
first aid given, record details:. . . . .   name of first aider:. . . . .

WITNESSES
name(s):. . . . .   address:. . . . .
postcode:. . . . .   telephone number:. . . . .
details recorded in the accident record book? . . . .
signature of injured person: . . . .   signature of first aider: . . . .
signature of witness: . . . .   signature of witness:. . . . .
signature of supervisor:. . . . .

An accident report form

HEALTH AND SAFETY

Breakages and spillages
When dealing with hazardous breakages and spillages, the hands should always be protected with gloves. To avoid injury to others, broken glass should be put in a secure container prior to disposing of it in a waste bin.

Accidents can damage stock, resulting in breakage of containers and spillage of contents. Breakage of glass can cause cuts; spillages can cause somebody to slip and fall. Any breakages or spillages should therefore be dealt with immediately and in the correct way.

You must determine whether the spillage is a potential hazard to health and what action is necessary. To whom should you report it? What equipment is required to remove the spillage? How should the materials be disposed of?

Always remember COSHH and check to see how the product should be handled and disposed of.

Reporting of Injuries, Diseases and Dangerous Occurrences Regulations (RIDDOR) (1995)

These require the employer to notify the local enforcement officer, in writing, when employees suffer personal injury at work. If this results in death, major injury or more than 24 hours in hospital, it must be reported by telephone first and followed by a written report within 7 days. In all cases of personal injury, an entry must be made in the workplace accident book. The information helps the Health and Safety Executive to investigate serious accidents.

First aid

The **Health and Safety (First Aid) Regulations (1981)** state that employers must have appropriate and adequate first aid arrangements in the event of an accident or illness.

All employees must be told of the first aid procedures, including:

- where to find the first aid box
- who is responsible for maintaining the first aid box
- which member of staff to inform in the event of an accident or illness
- which staff member to informing the event of an accident or emergency.

An adequately stocked first aid box should be available. As a minimum, this should contain:

- a basic first aid guidance leaflet (1)
- assorted sterile adhesive dressing (20)
- individually wrapped triangular bandages (6)
- safety pins (6)
- sterile eye pads, with attachments (2)
- medium-sized individually wrapped sterile unmedicated wound dressings 10 cm x 8 cm (6)
- large individually wrapped sterile unmedicated wound dressings 13 cm x 9 cm (2)
- extra large individually wrapped sterile unmedicated wound dressings 28 cm x 17.5 cm (3)
- individually wrapped medical wipes
- antiseptic cream or liquid

First aid equipment

Sterile water in sealed containers should be available to bathe the eyes if tap water is not readily available.

General guidance on first aid

Normally a casualty should be seated, or lying down, when being treated by a first aider.

Mouth-to-mouth resuscitation procedure

- Place the casualty on their back. Open and clear their mouth.
- Tilt head backwards to open airway (maintain this position throughout). Support the jaw.
- Kneel beside casualty, while keeping head backwards. Open mouth and pinch nose.
- Open you mouth and take deep breath. Seal their mouth with yours and breathe firmly into it. Casualty's chest should rise. Remove your mouth and let their chest fall. If their chest does not rise, check their head is tilted sufficiently. Repeat at a a rate of 10 times a minute until the casualty is breathing alone.
- Place them in a recovery position.

Further examples of first aid procedures

Problem	Action to be taken
Casualty is not breathing	1 Place the casualty on their back. Open and clear their mouth.
	2 Tilt head backwards to open airway (maintain this position throughout). Support the jaw.
	3 Kneel beside casualty, while keeping head backwards. Open mouth and pinch nose.
	4 Open your mouth and take a deep breath. Seal mouth with yours and breathe firmly into it. Casualty's chest should rise. Remove your mouth and let their chest fall. If chest does not rise, check head is tilted sufficiently. Repeat at a rate of 10 times a minute until the casualty is breathing alone.
	5 Place them in the recovery position.
Unconscious	Place into recovery position.
Severe bleeding	Control by direct pressure using fingers and thumb on the bleeding point. Apply a dressing. Raising the bleeding limb (unless it is broken) will reduce the flow of blood.
Suspected broken bones	Do not move the casualty unless they are in a position which exposes them to immediate danger.
Burns and scalds (due to heat)	Do not remove clothing sticking to the burns or scalds. Do not burst any blisters. If burns and scalds are small, flush them with plenty of clean, cool water before applying a sterilised dressing. If burns and scalds are large or deep, wash your hands, apply a dry sterilise dressing and send the casualty to hospital.

Problem	Action to be taken
Burns (chemicals)	Avoid contaminating yourself with the chemical. Remove any contaminated clothing which is not stock to skin. Flush with plenty of cool water for 10–15 minutes. Apply a sterilised dressing and send to hospital.
Foreign body in eye	Wash out eye with clean cool water. (A person with an eye injury should be sent to hospital with the eye covered with an eye pad.)
Chemicals in eyes	Wash out the open eye continuously with clean, cool water for 10–15 minutes.
Electric shock	Don't touch the casualty until the current is switched off. If the current cannot be switched off, stand on some dry insulating material and use a wooden or plastic implement to free the casualty from the electrical source. If breathing has stopped start mouth-to-mouth breathing and continue until the casualty starts to breathe by themselves or until professional help arrives.
Gassing	Use suitable protective equipment. Move casualty to fresh air. If breathing has stopped start mouth-to-mouth breathing and continue until the casualty is breathing himself or until professional help arrives. Send to hospital with a note of the gas involved.
Minor injuries	Casualties with minor injuries of a nature they would normally attend to themselves may wash their hands and apply a small sterilised dressing from the first aid box.

Disposal of waste

Waste should be disposed of in an enclosed waste bin fitted with a polythene bin liner that is durable enough not to tear. The bin should be sanitised regularly with disinfectant in a well-ventilated area: wear protective gloves when doing this. Hazardous waste must be disposed of following the COSHH procedures and employees should be trained in these.

Contaminated waste, such as wax strips, should be disposed of as recommended by your local authority. Items that have been used to pierce the skin, such as disposable milia extractors, should be discarded in a disposable **sharps container**. Again, contact your local authority to check on disposal arrangements.

Inspection and registration of premises

Local authority Environmental Health departments enforce the Health and Safety at Work Act and an **officer** authorised by the local authority visits and inspects local business premises. If the officer identifies an area of danger an **improvement notice** will be issued and it is the employer's responsibility to remove the danger within a designated period of time. Failure to comply with the notice will lead to prosecution. The inspector also has the authority to close a business until he or she is satisfied that all danger to employees and public has been removed. Such closure involves issuing a **prohibition notice**.

Certain treatments carried out in beauty therapy, such as ear piercing, pose additional risk because they might produce blood and body tissue fluid. Inspection of the premises is necessary before such services can be offered to the public. The inspector will visit to make sure that the guidelines listed in the **Local Government (Miscellaneous Provisions) Act (1982)** relating to this area are being complied with. When the inspector is satisfied, a certificate of registration will be awarded.

Fire

The **Fire Precautions Act (1971)** states that all staff must be aware of and trained in fire and emergency evacuation procedures for their workplace. The **emergency exit route** will be the easiest route by which staff the clients can leave the building safely.

A **fire certificate** is a compulsory requirement of the Act if there are more than 20 employees, or if more than 10 employees are on different floors at any one time.

The Fire Precautions (Workplace) Regulations (1997)

These require every employer to carry out a risk assessment for the premises, under the **Management of Health and Safety Regulations (1999)**:

- Any obstacles that might hinder fire evacuation should be identified as problems areas.
- Suitable fire detection equipment should be in place, such as a **smoke alarm**.
- A method to warn of a fire should be in place, this might be an automatic alarm or trained employee shouting to raise the alarm.
- All escape routes should be clearly marked and free from obstacles.
- Fire-fighting equipment should be available and maintained, to be used only by those trained in its use.
- All employees should be trained in fire-evacuation practice and procedures.
- Fire-evacuation procedures should be reviewed regularly to account for changes to the staffing or premises. A fire drill should be carried out at least once a year to monitor evacuation procedures.

Fire-fighting equipment

Fire-fighting equipment must be available, located in a specified area. The equipment includes fire extinguishers, blankets, sand buckets and water hoses. Fire-fighting equipment should be used only when the cause of the fire has been identified – using the fire *wrong* extinguisher could make the fire worse. Different types of fire extinguishers are available to tackle different types of fire and colour coded according to type.

ACTIVITY

Fire drill
Each workplace should have a fire drill regularly. This enables staff to practise so that they know what to do in the event of a real fire. What is the fire drill procedure to your workplace?

HEALTH AND SAFETY

Fire!
A fire can quickly get out of control. You do not have very long to act!
Fire drill notices should be visible to show people to the emergency exit route.
If there is a fire, never use a lift.

HEALTH AND SAFETY

Fire exits
Fire exit doors must be clearly marked, be unlocked during working hours and be free from obstruction.

ACTIVITY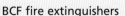

Fire extinguishers
Colour and symbols indicate the use of particular fire extinguishers. Make sure you know the meaning of each of the colours and symbols.

Cause of fire	Extinguisher type	Colour code
Electrical fire	Carbon dioxide (CO2)	Black
Solid material fire	Water	Red
Flammable liquids	Foam	Yellow
Vaporising liquids	BCF Green Dry-powder	Blue

Note: green and blue extinguishers can be used with all types of fire except flammable metal fires.

HEALTH AND SAFETY +

BCF fire extinguishers
BCF fire extinguishers – suitable for burning liquid and electrical fires – produce vapours that cut off the oxygen supply to the fire. This is dangerous to people when used in a confined space and although still available, these extinguishers are no longer manufactured in the EU.

It is important that you never use fire-fighting equipment unless you have been trained in its use.

Chubb Fire Ltd

Fire extinguisher symbols

Chubb Fire Ltd

Fire extinguishers

Fire blankets are used to smother a small, localised fire or if a person's clothing is on fire. **Sand** is used to soak up liquids if these are the source of the fire, and to smother the fire. **Water hoses** are used to extinguish large fires caused by paper materials and the like – buckets of water can be used to extinguish a small fire. *Turn off the electricity first!*

Other emergencies

Other possible emergencies that could occur relate to fumes and flooding. Learn the location of the water and gas stopcocks. In the event of a gas leak or a flood, the stopcocks should be switched off and the appropriate emergency service contacted.

Staff should also be trained in the procedures necessary for a bomb alert. This will involve recognising a suspect package, dealing with a bomb threat, evacuating staff and clients, and contacting the emergency services. Your local Crime Prevention Officer will advise on bomb security.

Chubb Fire Ltd

Fire blanket

Insurance

Public liability insurance protects employers and employees against the consequences of death or injury to a third party while on the premises.

Product and **treatment liability insurance** is usually included with your public liability insurance but it is worth checking this with the insurance company.

All employers must have **employer's liability insurance**. This provides financial compensation to an employee who is injured as a result of a workplace accident.

ACTIVITY

Causes of fires
Think of several potential causes of fire in the salon. How could each of these be prevented?

PERSONAL HEALTH, HYGIENE AND APPEARANCE

Your appearance enables the client to make an initial judgement about both you and the salon, so make sure that you create the right impression! Employees in the workplace should always reflect the desired image of the profession they work in.

HEALTH AND SAFETY ✚

Drugs
If you take drugs, how might his affect your responsibilities under the implementation of the health and safety policy of your workplace?

Professional appearance

Assistant therapist

Assistant therapists qualified to pre-foundation level will be required to wear a clean protective overall because they will be preparing the working area for client treatments and might also be involved in preparing clients.

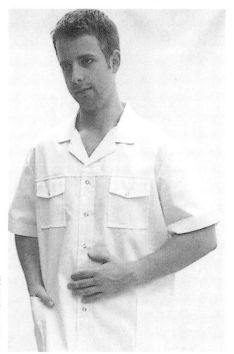

Your appearance must create the right impression at all times

Beauty therapist

The nature of many of the services offered requires beauty therapists to wear protective, hygienic clothing. A cotton overall is ideal; air can circulate, allowing perspiration to evaporate and discouraging body odour. Using a light colour such as white immediately shows the client that you are clean. A cotton overall might comprise a dress, a jumpsuit or a tunic top, with coordinating trousers.

Overalls should be laundered regularly and a fresh, clean overall worn each day.

Receptionist

A receptionist employed solely to carry out reception duties might wear a different salon dress, complementary to those worn by the practising therapists. As the receptionist will not be as active, a smart jacket or cardigan might be appropriate. However, if the receptionist also carries out client services, the standard salon overall must be worn.

General rules for employees

Make-up

Wear an attractive make-up, if worn, and use the correct skin-care cosmetics to suit your skin type. A healthy complexion will be a positive advertisement for your work.

Jewellery

Keep jewellery to a minimum, such as a wedding ring, a watch and small earrings.

Nails

Nails should be short, neatly manicured and free of nail polish unless the employee's main duties involve nail treatments or reception duties. Flesh-coloured tights can be worn to protect the legs.

Shoes

Wear flat, well-fitting, comfortable shoes that enclose the feet and complement the overall. Remember that you will be on your feet for most of the day!

Ethics

Beauty therapy has a **code of ethics**. Although not a legal requirement, this code can be used in criminal proceedings as evidence of improper practice.

ACTIVITY

Personal Appearance
Collect pictures from various suppliers of overalls. Select those that you feel would be most practical for an assistant therapist (a Level 1 beauty therapist). Briefly describe why you feel these are the most suitable.
Design various hairstyles, or collect pictures from magazines, to show how the hair could be smartly worn by a therapist with medium-length to long hair.

Diet, exercise and sleep

A beauty therapist requires stamina and energy. To achieve this you need to eat a healthy, well-balanced diet, take regular exercise and have enough sleep.

Posture

Posture is the way you hold yourself when standing, sitting and walking. *Correct* posture enables you to work longer without becoming tired, it prevents muscle fatigue and stiff joints, and it improves your appearance.

Good standing posture

If you are standing with good posture, this will describe you:

- head up, centrally balanced
- shoulders slightly back, and relaxed
- chest up and out
- abdomen flat
- hips level
- fingertips level
- bottom in
- knees level
- feet slightly apart and weight evenly distributed.

Good sitting posture

Sit on a suitable chair or stool with a good back support:

- sit with the lower back pressed against the chair back
- keep the chest up and the shoulders back
- distribute the body weight evenly along the thighs
- keep the feet together, and flat on the floor
- do not slouch, or sit on the edge of your seat.

ACTIVITY

Building stamina
Ask your tutor for guidelines before beginning this activity. Write down all the foods and drinks that you most enjoy. Are they healthy? If you are unsure, ask your tutor.
How much exercise do you take weekly?
How much sleep do you regularly have each night?
Do you think you could improve your health and fitness levels?

ACTIVITY

The importance of posture
Which treatments will be performed sitting, and which standing?
In what way do you feel your treatments would be affected if you were not sitting or standing correctly?

Good posture – sitting

Good posture – standing

ACTIVITY

Hand hygiene
What further occasions can you think of when it will be necessary to wash your hands when treating a client?

HEALTH AND SAFETY

Soap and towels
Wash your hands with liquid soap from a sealed dispenser. Don't refill disposable soap dispensers when empty: if you do they will become a breeding ground for bacteria.
Disposable paper towels or warm-air hand dryers should be used to dry the hands.

HEALTH AND SAFETY

Protecting yourself
You will be wise to have the relevant inoculations, including those against tetanus and hepatitis, to protect yourself against ill health and even death.

TIP

Fresh breath
When working, avoid eating strong-smelling highly spiced food.

HEALTH AND SAFETY

Long hair
If long hair is not taken away from the face, the tendency will be to move the hair away from the face repeatedly with the hands, and this in turn will require that the hands be washed repeatedly.

Personal hygiene

It is vital that you have a high standard of personal **hygiene**. You are going to be working in close proximity with people. Bodily cleanliness is achieved through daily showering or bathing. This removes the stale sweat, dirt and bacteria that cause body odour. An antiperspirant or deodorant could be applied to the underarm area to reduce perspiration and thus the smell of sweat. Clean underwear should be worn each day.

Hands

Your hands and everything you touch are covered with germs. Although most are harmless, some can cause ill health or disease. Wash your hands regularly, especially after you have been to the toilet and before eating food. You must also wash your hands before and after treating each client, and during treatment if necessary. Washing the hands before treating a client minimises the risk of cross-infection and presents a hygienic, professional and caring image to the client.

HEALTH AND SAFETY

Protecting the client
If you have any cuts or abrasions on your hands, cover them with a clean dressing to minimise the risk of secondary infection. Disposable gloves may be worn for additional protection.
Certain skin disorders are contagious. If the therapist is suffering from any such disorder she must not work, but must seek medical advice immediately.

Feet

Keep your feet fresh and healthy by washing them daily and then drying them thoroughly. Deodorising foot powder could then be applied.

Teeth

Avoid bad breath by brushing your teeth at least twice and day and flossing them regularly. Use breath fresheners and mouthwashes as required to freshen your breath. Visit the dentist regularly, to maintain healthy teeth and gums.

Hair

Your hair should be clean and tidy. Have your hair cut regularly and shampoo and condition it as often as needed. If your hair is long, wear it off the face and taken to the crown of the head. Medium-length hair should be clipped back, away from the face, to prevent it falling forwards.

Hygiene in the workplace

Infections

Effective salon hygiene is necessary to prevent *cross-infection* and *secondary infection*. These can occur through poor practice, such as the use of implements that are not sterile. Infection can be recognised by the skin being red and inflamed, or pus being present.

Cross-infection occurs because some micro-organisms are contagious, that is, they can be transferred through personal contact – by touch or by contact with an infected instrument that has not been sterilised. **Secondary infection** can occur as a result of injury to the client during the treatment or, if the client already has an open cut, if bacteria penetrate the skin and cause infection. **Sterilisation** and **sanitisation** procedures (see below) are used to minimise or destroy the harmful micro-organisms that could cause infection.

Infectious contagious diseases **contra-indicate** beauty treatment: they require medical attention. People with certain other skin disorders, even though these are not contagious, should likewise not be treated by the beauty therapist, as treatment might lead to secondary infection.

Sterilisation and sanitisation

- **Sterilisation** is the total destruction of all living micro-organisms.
- **Sanitisation** is the destruction of some, but not all, micro-organisms.

Sterilisation and sanitisation techniques practised in the beauty salon involve the use of *physical* agents (e.g. radiation and heat) and *chemical* agents (e.g. antiseptics and disinfectants).

Radiation

A quartz mercury vapour lamp can be used as the source for **ultraviolet light**, which destroys micro-organisms. The object to be sanitised must be turned regularly so that the ultraviolet light reaches all surfaces. (Remember that ultraviolet light is of limited effectiveness and cannot be relied upon for sterilisation.)

The ultraviolet lamp must be contained within a closed cabinet. This cabinet is an ideal place for storing sterilised objects.

Heat

Dry and moist heat can both be used in sterilisation. One method is to use a dry **hot-air oven**. This is similar to a small oven, and heats to 150–180°C. It is seldom used in the salon.

More practical is a **glass-bead steriliser**. This is a small, electrically heated unit that contains glass beads: these transfer heat to objects placed in contact with them. This method of sterilisation is suitable for small tools such as tweezers and scissors.

ACTIVITY

Preventing the spread of infection
Think of different ways in which infection could be spread in the salon. In each case, what could be done to prevent the spread?

Sonisa

An ultra-voilet light cabinet

HEALTH AND SAFETY

Sterilisation record
Ultraviolet light is dangerous, especially to the eyes. The lamp must be switched off before opening the cabinet. A record must be kept of usage, as the effectiveness of the lamp decreases with use.

Using an autoclave
Not all objects can safely be placed in the autoclave. Before using this method, check whether the items you wish to sterilise can withstand this heating process.
To avoid damaging the autoclave, always use distilled deionised water.
To avoid rusting, metal objects placed in the sterilising unit must be of good-quality stainless steel.

HEALTH AND SAFETY

Using disinfectant
Disinfectant solutions should be changed as necessary.
After removing the object from the disinfectant, rinse it in clean water to remove traces of the solution. These might otherwise cause an allergic reaction on the client's skin.

Ellisons

Sterilisation tray with liquid

TIP

Surgical spirit
Before sterilisation, surgical spirit may be used to clean small objects.

Water is boiled in an **autoclave** (similar to a pressure cooker): because of the increased pressure, the water reaches a temperature of 121–134°C. Autoclaving is the most effective method for sterilising objects in the salon.

Gases

Gases used in sterilising include **ethylene oxide** and **formaldehyde**. These chemicals are hazardous to handle and are therefore unpopular.

Depilex

An autoclave

Disinfectants and antiseptics

If an object cannot be sterilised, it should be placed in a chemical **disinfectant** solution such as **quaternary ammonium compounds** (**quats**) or **glutaraldehyde**. A disinfectant destroys most micro-organisms, but not all.

An **antiseptic** prevents the multiplication of micro-organisms. It has a limited action and does not kill all micro-organisms. Because it is milder than a disinfectant, it can be used directly on the skin.

All sterilisation techniques must be carried out safely and effectively:

1 Select the appropriate method of sterilisation for the object. Always follow the manufacturer's guidelines on the use of the sterilising unit or agent.

2 Clean the object in clean water and detergent to remove dirt and grease. (Dirt left on the object might prevent effective sterilisation.)

3 Dry the object thoroughly with a clean, disposable paper towel.

4 Sterilise the object, allowing sufficient time for the process to be completed.

5 Place tools that have been sterilised in a clean, covered container.

Keep several sets of the tools you use regularly, so that you can carry out effective sterilisation.

General salon hygiene rules

- Health and safety: follow the health and safety guidelines for the workplace.
- Personal hygiene: maintain a high standard of personal hygiene. Wash your hands with a detergent containing **chlorhexidine**.
- Cuts on the hands: always cover any cuts on your hands.
- Cross-infection: take great care to avoid cross-infection in the salon. Never treat a client who has a contagious skin disease or disorder, or any other contraindication.
- Use hygienic tools: never use an implement unless it has been effectively sterilised or sanitised, as appropriate.
- Disposable products: wherever possible, use disposable products.

- Working surfaces: clean all working surfaces (such as trolleys and couches) with a chlorine preparation, diluted to the manufacturer's instructions. Cover all working surfaces with clean, disposable paper tissue.
- Gowns and towels: clean gowns and towels must be provided for each client.
- Laundry: dirty laundry should be placed in a covered container.
- Waste: put waste in a suitable container lined with a disposable waste bag. A yellow '**sharps' container** should be available for waste contaminated with blood or tissue fluid.
- Eating and drinking; never eat or drink in the treatment area of the salon.

SKIN DISEASES AND DISORDERS

The beauty therapist must be able to distinguish a healthy skin from one suffering from a skin disease or disorder. Certain skin disorders and diseases **contra-indicate** a beauty treatment: the treatment would expose the therapist and other clients to the risk of cross-infection. It is therefore vital that you are familiar with the skin diseases and disorders with which you might come into contact in the workplace. You will find further information relevant to the treatment area in Chapters 4 and 5.

Bacterial infections

Bacteria are minute single-celled organisms of varied shapes. Large numbers of bacteria inhabit the surface of the skin and are harmless (**non-pathogenic**); indeed some play an important positive role in the health of the skin. Others, however, are harmful (**pathogenic**) and can cause skin diseases. Bacterial infections include:

- Impetigo: an inflammatory disease of the surface of the skin.
- Conjunctivitis or pink eye: inflammation of the mucous membrane that covers the eye and lines the eyelids.
- Hordeola or styes: infection of the sebaceous glands of eyelash hair follicles.
- Furuncles or boils: red, painful lumps, extending deeply into the skin.
- Carbuncles: infection of numerous hair follicles.
- Paronychia: infection of the tissue surrounding the nail.

ACTIVITY

To see images of skin diseases and disorders you could search on the internet.

ACTIVITY

Avoiding cross-infection
List the different ways in which
infection can be transferred in
the salon.
How can you avoid cross-
infection in the workplace?

Viral infections

Viruses are minute entities, too small to see even under an ordinary
microscope. Viruses invade healthy body cells and multiply within the cell: in
due course the cell walls break down, liberating new viral particles to attack
further cells, and thus the infection spreads.

- Herpes simplex: a recurring skin condition, appearing at times when the
  skin's resistance is lowered through ill health or stress. It might also be
  caused by exposure of the skin to extremes of temperature or to ultraviolet
  light.
- Herpes zoster or shingles: in this painful disease, the virus attacks the
  sensory nerve endings. The virus is thought to lie dormant in the body and
  be triggered when the body's defences are at a low ebb.
- Verrucae or warts: small epidermal skin growths. Warts can be raised or flat,
  depending upon their position. There are several types of wart: plane,
  common and plantar.

Infestations

- Scabies or itch mites: a condition in which an animal parasite burrows
  beneath the skin and invades the hair follicles.
- Pediculosis capitis or head lice: a condition in which small parasites infest
  scalp hair.
- Pediculosis pubis: a condition in which small parasites infest body hair.
- Pediculosis corporis: a condition in which small parasites live and feed on
  body skin.

Fungal diseases

Fungi are microscopic plants. They depend on their host for their existence.
Fungal diseases of the skin feed off the waste products of the skin. Some fungi
are found on the skin's surface; others attack the deeper tissues. Reproduction
of fungi is by means of simple cell division or by the production of spores.

- Tinea pedis or athlete's foot: a common fungal foot infection.
- Tinea corporis or body ringworm: a fungal infection of the skin.
- Tinea unguium: ringworm infection of the fingernails.

Sebaceous gland disorders

The sebaceous glands are minute, sac-like organs in the skin. The cells of the
glands produce the skin's natural oil – sebum.

- Milia: keratinisation of the skin over the hair follicle occurs, causing sebum to
  accumulate in the hair follicle. This condition usually accompanies dry skin.

- Comedones or blackheads: excess sebum and keratinised cells block the mouth of the hair follicle.

- Seborrhoea: excessive secretion of sebum from the sebaceous gland. This usually occurs during puberty, as a result of hormonal changes in the body.

- Steatomas, sebaceous cysts or wens: localised pockets or sacs of sebum that form in hair follicles or under the sebaceous glands in the skin. The sebum becomes stuck, the sebaceous gland becomes distended and a lump forms.

- Acne vulgaris: hormone imbalance in the body at puberty influences the activity of the sebaceous gland, causing an increased production of sebum. The sebum can be retained within the sebaceous ducts, causing congestion and bacterial infection of the surrounding tissues.

- Acne rosacea: excessive sebum secretion combined with a chronic inflammatory condition, caused by dilation of the blood capillaries.

Pigmentation disorders

Pigmentation of the skin varies, according to the person's genetic characteristics. In general, the darker the skin, the more pigment is present, but some abnormal changes in skin pigmentation can occur:

- **Hyperpigmentation**: increased pigment production
- **Hypopigmentation**: loss of pigmentation in the skin.
- Ephelides or freckles: multiple, small pigmented areas of the skin. Exposure to ultraviolet light (as in sunlight) stimulates the production of melanin, intensifying their appearance.
- Lentigines: pigmented areas of skin, slightly larger than freckles, which do not darken on exposure to ultraviolet light.
- Chloasmata or liver spots: increased skin pigmentation in specific areas, stimulated by a skin irritant such as ultraviolet light. The condition often occurs during pregnancy and usually disappears soon after the birth of the baby. It might also occur as a result of taking the oral contraceptive pill. The female hormone oestrogen is thought to stimulate melanin production.
- Dermatosis papulosa nigra: often called flesh moles; characterised by multiple benign, small brown to black hyperpigmented papules, common in people with dark skins.
- Vitiligo of leucoderma: patches of completely white skin that have lost their pigment, or which were never pigented.
- Albinism: the skin is unable to produce melanin and the skin, hair and eyes lack colour.
- Vascular naevi: there are two types of naevus of concern to beauty therapists: vascular and cellular. Vascular naevi are skin conditions in which small or large areas of skin pigmentation are caused by the permanent dilation of blood capillaries.
- Erythema: an area of skin in which blood capillaries have dilated, due either to injury or inflammation.
- Dilated capillaries: capillaries near the surface of the skin are permanently dilated.

TIP

Hyperpigmentation
Hyperpigmentation may result from certain skin injuries, disorders or diseases.

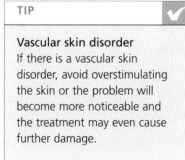

TIP

Vascular skin disorder
If there is a vascular skin disorder, avoid overstimulating the skin or the problem will become more noticeable and the treatment may even cause further damage.

- Spider naevi or stellate haemangiomas: dilated blood vessels, with smaller dilated capillaries radiating from them.
- Naevi vasculosis or strawberry marks: red or purplish raised marks that appear on the skin at birth.
- Capillary naevi or port-wine stains: large areas of dilated capillaries that contrast noticeably with the surrounding areas.
- Cellular naevi or moles: skin conditions in which changes in the cells of the skin result in skin malformations.
- Malignant melanomas or malignant moles: rapidly growing skin cancers, usually occurring in adults.
- Junction naevi: localised collections of naevoid cells that arise from the mass production locally of pigment-forming cells (melanocytes).
- Dermal naevi: localised collections of naevoid cells.
- Hairy naevi: moles exhibiting coarse hairs from their surface.

HEALTH AND SAFETY

Moles
If moles change in shape or size, if they bleed or form crusts, seek medical attention.

Skin disorders involving abnormal growth

- Psoriasis: patches of itchy, red, flaky skin, the cause of which is unknown.
- Seborrhoeic or senile warts: raised, pigmented, benign tumours occurring in middle age.
- Verrucae filliformis or skin tags: these verrucae appear as threads projecting from the skin.
- Xanthomas: small, yellow growths on the surface of the skin.
- Keloids: these occur after skin injury. They are overgrown abnormal scar tissues, which spread and are characterised by excess deposits of collagen. To avoid skin discoloration the keloid must be protected from exposure to ultraviolet light.

HEALTH AND SAFETY

Skin Tags
Skin tags often occur under the arms. In case they are present, take care when carrying out a wax depilation treatment in this area: do not apply wax over tags.

Malignant (harmful) tumours

- Squamous cell carcinomas or prickle-cell cancers: malignant growths originating in the epidermis.
- Basal cell carcinomas or rodent ulcers: slow-growing malignant tumours that occur in middle age.

Skin allergies

HEALTH AND SAFETY

Record any known allergies
When completing the client record card, always ask whether your client has any known allergies.

The skin can protect itself – to some degree – from damage or invasion. Any damage that occurs is detected by specialised **mast cells** that release the chemical **histamine** into the tissues. Histamine causes the blood capillaries to dilate, producing the reddening we call 'erythema'. The increased blood flow through these dilated capillaries brings materials in blood to the site of injury; these act to limit the damage and begin the process of repair.

If the skin is sensitive to and becomes inflamed on contact with a particular substance, this substance is called an **allergen**. Allergens can be animal, chemical or vegetable substances, and they can be inhaled, eaten or absorbed after contact with the skin. An **allergic skin reaction** appears as irritation, itching and discomfort, with reddening and swelling (as with nettle rash). It the allergen is removed, the allergic reaction subsides.

Everyone has different tolerances to the various substances we encounter in daily life. What causes an allergic reaction in one individual might be perfectly harmless to another. The following are just a few examples of allergens known to cause allergic skin reactions:

- metal objects containing nickel
- sticking plaster
- rubber
- lipstick containing eosin dye
- nail enamel containing formaldehyde resin
- hair and eyelash dyes
- lanolin, the skin moisturising agent
- detergents that dry the skin
- foods – well know examples are peanuts, cow's milk, lobster, shellfish and strawberries
- plants – such as tulips and chrysanthemums.
- Dermatitis: an inflammatory skin disorder in which the skin become red, itchy and swollen. There are two types of dermatitis. In *primary dermatitis* the skin is irritated by the action of a substance on the skin, and this leads to skin inflammation. In *allergic contact dermatitis*, the problem is caused by intolerance of the skin to a particular substance or groups of substances. On exposure to the substance the skin quickly becomes irritated and an allergic reaction occurs.
- Eczema: inflammation of the skin caused by contact, internally or externally, with an irritant.
- Urticaria (nettle rash) or hives: a minor skin disorder caused by contact with an allergen, either internally (e.g. food or drugs) or externally (e.g. insect bites).

HEALTH AND SAFETY

Hypoallergenic products
The use of hypoallergenic products minimises the risk of skin contact with likely irritants.

HEALTH AND SAFETY

Allergies
You may suddenly become allergic to a substance that has previously been perfectly harmless. Equally, you may over time cease to be allergic to something.

HEALTH AND SAFETY

Infection following allergy
Following an allergic skin reaction in which the skin's surface has become itchy and broken, scratching may cause the skin to become infected with bacteria.

Glossary

Autoclave	an effective method of sterilisation, suitable for small metal objects and beauty therapy tools. Water is boiled under increased pressure and reaches temperatures of 121–134°C
Bacteria	minute, single-celled organisms of various shapes. Large numbers live on the skins surface and are not harmful (non-pathogenic); others, however, are harmful (pathogenic) and can cause disease
Control of Substances Hazardous to Health (COSHH) (1999)	these regulations require employers to identify hazardous substances used in the workplace and state how they should be correctly store and handled
Cross-infection	the transfer of contagious micro-organisms
Disinfectant	a chemical agent that destroys most micro-organisms
Electricity at Work Regulations (1989)	these regulations state that electrical equipment in the workplace should be tested every 12 months, by a qualified electrician. The employer must keep records of the equipment tested and the date it was checked
Erythema	reddening of the skin
Fire Precautions (Workplace) Regulations (1997)	this legislation requires that every employer must carry out a risk assessment for the premises in relation to fire evacuation practice and procedures under the Management of Health and Safety Regulations (1999)
Fire Precautions Act (1971)	legislation that states that all staff must be familiar with and trained in fire and emergency evacuation procedures for their workplace
Fungus	microscopic plants. Fungal diseases of the skin feed of the waste products of the skin. They are found on the skins surface or the can attack deeper tissues
Hazard	a hazard is something with potential to cause harm
Health and safety (Display Screen Equipment) 1992	these regulations cover the use of visual display units (VDUs) and computer screens. They specify acceptable levels of radiation emissions from the screen and identify correct posture, seating position, permitted working heights and rest periods.
Health and Safety (First Aid) Regulations (1981)	legislation that states that workplaces must have appropriate and adequate first-aid provision

Glossary

Health and Safety at Work Act (1974)	legislation that lays down the minimum standards of health safety and welfare requirements in all workplaces
Histamine	a chemical released when the skin comes into contact with a substance that it is allergic to. Cells called mast cells burst, releasing histamine into the tissues. This causes the blood capillaries to dilate, which increases blood flow to limit skin damage and begin repair
Hygiene	the recommended standard of cleanliness necessary in the salon to prevent cross-infection
Hyperpigmentation	increased pigment production
Hypopigmentation	loss of pigmentation
Infestation	a condition where animal parasites live off and invade a host
Legislation	laws affecting the beauty therapy business relating to products and services, the business premises and environmental conditions, working practises and those employed
Management of Health and Safety at Work Regulations (1999)	this legislation provides the employer with an approved code of practice for maintaining a safe, secure working environment
Manual Handling Operations (1992)	legislation that requires the employer to carryout a risk assessment of all activities undertaken which involves manual handling (lifting and moving objects)
Personal Protective Equipment (PPE) at Work Regulations (1992)	this legislation requires employers to identify through risk assessment those activities that require special protective equipment to be worn.
Posture	the position of the body, which varies from person to person. Good posture is when the body is in alignment. Correct posture enables you to work longer without becoming tired; it prevents muscle fatigue and stiff joints.
Provision and Use of Work Equipment Regulations (PUWER) (1998)	this regulation lays down important health and safety controls on the provision and use of equipment

Glossary

Reporting of Injuries, Diseases and Dangerous Occurrences Regulations (RIDDOR) (1995)	these regulations require the employer to notify the local enforcement officer in writing, in cases where employees or trainees suffer personal injury at work.
Risk	a risk is the likelihood of the hazards potential being realised
Sanitisation	the destruction of some but not all micro-organisms
Secondary infection	bacterial penetration into the skin causing infection
Sterilisation	the destruction of all micro-organisms
Ultraviolet light (UVL) cabinet	a unit that uses ultraviolet light to sanitise small objects. Objects must be clean before placing in the cabinet, and must be turned so that the ultraviolet light rays effectively strike each surface of the object.
Virus	the smallest living bodies – too small to see under an ordinary microscope. Viruses invade healthy body cells and multiply within the cell. Eventually the cell walls break down and the virus particles are freed to attack further cells.
Workplace (Health Safety and Welfare) Regulations (1992)	these regulations provide the employer with an approved code of practice for maintaining a safe, secure working environment

Assessment and knowledge of understanding

Unit G1: Ensure your own actions reduce risks to health and safety (mandatory unit)

You have now learnt about the health and safety responsibilities for everyone in the workplace. This will enable you to ensure your own actions reduce risks to health and safety. To test your level of knowledge and understanding, answer the following short questions, these will prepare you for your summative (final) assessment.

Action to avoid health and safety risks:

1 What are your main legal responsibilities under the Health and Safety at Work Act (1974)?

2 Give five examples of good personal presentation in maintaining health and safety in the salon?

3 Why is your personal conduct important to maintain the health and safety of yourself and colleagues and clients?

4 Why must you always be aware of and look for hazards in the workplace?

5 What do you understand by these terms?
   a sterilisation
   b sanitisation

6 Name a piece of equipment that is used in the work place for sterilisation and sanitisation.

7 What do you understand by good posture, and why is it important for you to consider when working?

8 You have been asked to check the contents of the first aid box, what should it contain?

Dealing with significant risks in your workplace:

1 In your workplace, think of the main risks that could occur and what precautions you could take to safe guard yourself and others?

2 While cleaning a wax heater you notice that the wires in the lead are exposed. What action should you take?

3 If you were unable to deal with a risk (because it was outside your area of responsibility) what action would you take?

4 What does the abbreviation COSHH stand for? Why is it important to follow the supplier's and manufacturer's instructions for the safe use of materials and products?

5 When cleaning the area after wax depilation treatment, what personal protective equipment should you wear and how should waste be disposed of?

Assessment and knowledge of understanding

6 You notice that a large box containing stock has been left in front of a fire exit, why is it important that this is removed?

7 It is a heavy box but you will be able lift it. What is the correct lifting technique to lift an object from the ground?

Taking the right action in the event of a danger:

1 What is the procedure for dealing with an accident in the workplace?

2 What is a fire drill? What is the fire evacuation procedure in your workplace? How often should this be carried out?

3 In the event of a real fire, after having safely evacuated the building, how would you contact the appropriate emergency service?

4 In reception, you discover a smoking bin in which a fire has started because of an un-extinguished cigarette. How should this fire be extinguished?

5 What action should be taken in the event of a gas leak?

chapter 2

ASSIST WITH SALON RECEPTION DUTIES

G2

Learning objectives

This chapter covers the skills and knowledge you need to help with salon reception duties. These include maintaining the reception area in a clean and tidy manner, looking after clients on arrival and departure, dealing with enquiries and scheduling appointments. It describes the competencies to enable you to:

- maintain the reception area

- attend to clients and enquiries

- help to make appointments for salon services.

Ensure that the reception area is clean and tidy at all times

Ensure that product displays are clean, well-stocked and appealing to the eye at all times

Show good client care and hospitality

To maintain the reception area you should

Remove any faulty or damaged products and equipment from the reception area following health and safety best practice. Report immediately to the supervisor

Report shortages of reception resources, i.e. stationery, price lists or retail products to the supervisor

PRACTICAL SKILLS AND KNOWLEDGE CHECKLIST

The table shown will help you to check your progress in gaining the necessary practical skills and knowledge for Unit G2: Assist with salon reception duties.
Tick (✓), when you feel you have gained your practical skills and knowledge in the following areas:

	✓
1 Maintaining the reception area	
2 Maintaining reception product displays including the removal of any faulty products	
3 Knowing when and whom to report low levels of reception stationery and retail stock	
4 Salon policy for reception client hospitality	
5 Using good verbal and non-verbal communication and listening skills to suit the situation	
6 Dealing with enquiries efficiently and competently	
7 Knowing when to refer enquiries on and to whom	
8 How to accurately record messages taken and when to pass on information and to whom	
9 Legal storage and access of client records in relation to the Data Protection Act (1998)	
10 How to efficiently deal with requests for appointments face to face or by telephone	
11 Ensuring all appointments details are recorded legibly, correctly and confirmed for accuracy with the client as per salon policy	
12 Knowing when to refer appointment requests on and to whom	
13 To have a good understanding of salon services, products and pricings	

When you have ticked all the areas you can ask your assessor to assess you on unit G2: Assist with salon reception duties. After practical assessment, your assessor might decide that you need to practice further to improve your skills. If so, your assessor will tell you how and where you need to improve to gain competence.

INTRODUCTION

The salon **reception** gives clients their first (and also their final) impression of the salon, whether this is on the telephone or in person on a visit to the salon. First impressions count, so make sure that clients get the *right* impression!

THE RECEPTION AREA

It is your responsibility to keep the reception area looking tidy and organised, and to be organised and pleasant when assisting with reception duties.

Assist with salon reception duties

Keep the reception area clean and tidy
Display areas should be clean and well stocked

↓

Report shortages of reception resources and retail products

↓

Identify and inform supervisor of faulty or damaged
equipment and products

↓

Show good client care and hospitality at all times

↓

Refer any enquiries you are unable to deal with
to the relevant person

↓

Accurately take messages and pass these on promptly

↓

Comply with the Data Protection Act (1998)
regarding client records

↓

Handle appointments immediately,
accurately identify client requirements

↓

Record all details accurately in the correct place and confirm
appointment details with the client

↓

Refer any appointments you are unable to deal
with to the relevant person

TIP

Protect the floor
Have an attractive, heavy-duty mat at the entrance to reception to protect the main floor-covering. Vacuum the mat when necessary during the day to keep the reception looking attractive.

TIP

Video facilities
Video facilities in reception can be used to promote salon services. If your salon provides this facility, make sure video material is played regularly.

HEALTH AND SAFETY

Ventilation
If smoking is allowed in the reception area, to avoid losing the custom of non-smoking clients you will need to make sure that the air is fresh and the room adequately ventilated to remove the smell of stale tobacco.

CLIENT HOSPITALITY

Hospitality is important and shows the salon's commitment to client care. If a client arrives early for an appointment, or is likely to be delayed, offer a magazine or a refreshment such as coffee or water; magazines should be renewed regularly. It is also a pleasant gesture to have boiled sweets on reception for clients.

Smoking

Each salon determines its own smoking policy. If smoking is allowed in reception, adequate ashtrays should be provided. These should be emptied and cleaned after each use.

CLIENT RECORDS

The Data Protection Act (1998)

This legislation is designed to protect the client's privacy and confidentiality. It is necessary to ask the client questions before the treatment place can be finalised and the information obtained is recorded on the client record card. All information about a client is confidential and should be stored in a secure area following client treatment. This is usually at reception. When assisting with reception duties, you must only pass the client's confidential information to authorised people, and you must always store client records securely.

ACTIVITY

Planning a reception area
Design a reception area (to scale) appropriate to a small or large beauty salon. Discuss the choice of wall and floor coverings, furnishings and equipment, and give the reasons for their selection. Consider client comfort, and health and safety.

HEALTH AND SAFETY

Cleaning
A large salon might employ a cleaner to maintain the hygiene of the reception area. In a smaller salon this might be the responsibility of an apprentice, the receptionist or a therapist. Reception must be maintained to a high standard at all times.

THE RECEPTIONIST

Receptionists should have a smart appearance and be able to communicate effectively and professionally, thereby creating the right impression.

As an assistant receptionist, your duties include:

- maintaining the reception area
- looking after clients on arrival and departure
- assisting with scheduling appointments
- dealing with enquiries
- telling the appropriate therapist that a client or visitor has arrived
- assisting with retail sales within your level of responsibility.

TIP ✔

Wear a badge
It is a good idea for receptionists to wear a badge indicating their name and position.

TIP ✔

Be polite
If you are engaged on the telephone when a client arrives, look up and acknowledge the client's presence.

TIP ✔

Be careful not to interrupt
If you need to pass information to another beauty therapist, never interrupt a client service. Wait until a suitable point in the treatment to communicate. If urgent information needs to be passed on, do so with minimum disruption.

The assistant receptionist should know:

- the name of each member of staff, their role and their area of responsibility
- the salon's hours of opening, and the days and times when each therapist is available
- the range of services or products offered by the salon, and their cost
- who to refer to if you receive different enquiries that you are unable to deal with or are not within your area of responsibility
- the person in your salon to whom you should refer reception problems
- any current discounts and special offers that the salon is promoting
- the benefits of each treatment and each retail product
- the approximate time taken to complete each treatment
- how to schedule follow-up treatments.

You will also need to consider the last three points when completing Unit BT1: Prepare and maintain the beauty therapy work area.

Qualities of a receptionist

All clients should feel valued. The following verbal and non-verbal **communication skills** are desirable in a receptionist:

- the ability to act positively and confidently
- clear speech
- a friendly and smiling approach
- paying attention to the client and maintain eye contact
- good listening skills
- demonstrating interest in everything that is going on around the reception area
- giving each client individual attention and respect.

Dealing with a dissatisfied client at reception

Occasionally, a client might be dissatisfied. The receptionist is usually the first contact with the client and you might have to deal with dissatisfied, angry or awkward customers in a public place. Considerable skill is needed if you are to deal constructively with a potentially damaging situation.

Never become angry or awkward yourself. Always remain courteous and tactful, and communicate confidently and politely.

- Listen to the clients as they describe their problems, without making judgement. Do not make excuses for yourself or for colleagues.
- Ask questions to check that you have the full background details.
- If possible, agree on a course of action, offering a solution if you can. Check

that the client has agreed to the proposed course of action. It might be necessary to consult the salon manager before proposing a solution to the client: if you're not sure, always check first.

- Log the complaint following salon policy recording: the date, the time, the client's name, the nature of the complaint and the agreed course of action.

ACTIVITY

Do's and don'ts
List five important do's and five don'ts for the receptionist.

MAKING APPOINTMENTS

Making correct entries in the appointment book or salon computer is one of the most important duties of the receptionist. As assistant receptionist, you must familiarise yourself with the salon's appointment system, column headings, treatment times and any abbreviations used for the treatments.

Each beauty therapist will have her name at the head of a column. Entries in columns must not be reallocated without the consent of the therapist, unless she is absent, when a senior therapist would reallocate the client bookings to ensure minimum disruption.

Information required

When clients call to make an appointment, their name and the treatment service wanted should be recorded. Allow adequate time to carry out the required service. Take the client's telephone number in case the therapist falls ill or is unable to keep the appointment for some other reason. If the client requests a particular therapist, be sure to enter the client's name in the correct column.

The hours of the day are recorded along the left-hand side of the appointment page, divided into 15-minute intervals. You need to know how long each treatment takes so that you can allow sufficient time for the therapist to carry out the treatment in a safe, competent, professional manner. If you don't allow sufficient time, the therapist will run late and this will affect all later appointments. On the other hand, if you allow too much time, the therapist's time will be wasted and the salon's earnings will be less than they could be. Suggested times to be allowed for each service are given in the treatment chapters. See the table on the next page for a breakdown of treatments and their abbreviations and times allowed.

Confirm the name of the therapist who will be carrying out the treatment, the date and the time.

Finally, confirm or estimate the cost of the treatment to the client.

You could offer an **appointment card** to the client, to confirm the appointment. The card should record the treatment, the date, the day and the time. The therapist's name might also be recorded.

Treatments are usually recorded in an abbreviated form. Everyone who uses the appointment page must be familiar with these abbreviations.

ACTIVITY

Reception scenarios
With colleagues, consider the following situations that might occur when working as a receptionist. What would you do in each situation?
- A client arrives very late for an appointment but insists that she is treated.
- A client questions the bill.
- A client comes in to complain about a treatment given previously.

HEALTH AND SAFETY

Health and safety (display screen equipment) regulations (1992)
These regulations cover the use of visual display units (VDUs) and computer screens. They specify acceptable levels of radiation emissions from the screen and identify correct posture, seating position, permitted working heights and rest periods.

Treatment service timings

Treatment	Abbreviation	Treatment time allowed
Cleanse and make-up	C/M/up	45 minutes
Eyebrow shaping	E/B reshape or trim	15 minutes
Eyebrow tint	EBT	10 minutes
Eyelash tint	ELT	20 minutes
Eyelash perm	ELP	45 minutes
Manicure	Man	45 minutes
Nail art	N/Art	5–10 minutes (per nail)
Pedicure	Ped	45 minutes
Waxing:	half	$^1/_2$ leg wax 30 minutes
	three-quarter	$^3/_4$ leg wax 30–40 minutes
	full	Full leg wax 50 minutes
Bikini wax	B/wax	15 minutes
Underarm wax	U/arm wax	15 minutes
Forearm wax	F/arm wax	30 minutes
Eyebrow wax	E/B wax	15 minutes
Ear pierce	E/P	15 minutes
Facial	F	60 minutes
False lashes	F/Lash	20 minutes

Treatment abbreviations and times allowed for various treatment

When making appointments for salon services you must

- Acknowledge the client immediately especially in busy trading conditions or answer the call promptly if an appointment is made over the phone
- Ensure the client is informed of any specific treatment information, e.g. the necessity of a skin test prior to permanent tinting
- Refery any enquiry that you cannot deal with yourself to the releveant person promptly
- Provide the client presenting in person with an appointment card confirming details of the appointment booking
- Ensure when making an appointment that you:
  - Record the name of the client treatment using the appropriate abbreviation in the correct place
  - Take client's contact telephone no.
  - Allow sufficient time
  - Confirm all details with the client

If an appointment book is used, write each entry neatly and accurately. It is preferable to write in pencil: appointments can be amended by erasing and rewriting, keeping the book clean and clear.

Appointments can be made up to 6 weeks in advance. Often, clients will book their next appointment as they leave the current appointment. How far ahead the receptionist is able to book appointments will vary from salon to salon.

When clients arrive for their treatment, draw a line (or tick) through their name to indicate that they have arrived.

DAY SATURDAY		DATE 17th MARCH	
THERAPIST	JANE	SUE	LIZ
9.00	Mrs Young		
9.15	½ Leg wax	Jenny Heron	
9.30	Carol Green	ELT DEBT	
9.45	Full Leg wax	Hair trim	
10.00	B / wax		
10.15		Sandra Smith	Fiona Smith
10.30	Mrs Lord E/B wax	C / M / UP	C / M / UP
10.45			strip lash
11.00		Mrs James	
11.15		u/arm wax	
11.30		f/arm wax	Carol Brown
11.45	////		DNA ELT
12.00			
12.15			
12.30	Jeanette Raffell		
12.45	man .	///	
1.00	ped.		
1.15		Sue Yip E/P	
1.30	½ Leg wax	T. Scott	///
1.45		¾ Leg wax	
2.00	Liz Whiteside	u/arm wax	
2.15	facial		
2.30			
2.45			Pat King
3.00			C / M / UP
3.15	Ann Wood		man.
3.30	man ,		
3.45	E/B Reshape		
4.00			

An appointment page from the appointment book

PRACTICAL SKILLS AND KNOWLEDGE CHECKLIST

The table shown will help you to check your progress in gaining the necessary practical skills and knowledge for Unit BT1: Prepare and maintain the beauty therapy area.
Tick (✓), when you feel you have gained your practical skills and knowledge in the following areas:

	✓
1 The environmental conditions for **each** treatment, including: ● lighting ● heating ● ventilation ● general comfort	
2 Selecting and using the correct method of sanitisation/sterilisation for tools and equipment required	
3 Preparing the treatment area for **waxing** following all health and safety requirements	
4 Preparing the treatment area for **eye treatments** following all health and safety requirements	
5 Preparing the treatment area for **make-up** following all health and safety requirements	
6 Preparing the treatment area for **manicure** following all health and safety requirements	
7 Preparing the treatment area for **pedicure** following all health and safety requirements	
8 Preparing the treatment area for **facial treatment** following all health and safety requirements	
9 Personal presentation and hygiene is maintained at all times	
10 Positive communication skills are used when liaising with clients and colleagues	
11 Obtaining clients records efficiently	
12 Methods of waste removal and disposal	
13 Manufacturers guidelines for the care and maintenance of equipment	
14 Cleaning and tidying the work ready for further treatments	
15 Storage of client records following treatment	

When you have ticked all the areas you can ask your assessor to assess you on Unit BT1: Prepare and maintain the beauty therapy work area. After practical assessment, your assessor might decide that you need more practice to improve your skills. If so, your assessor will tell you how and where you need to improve to gain competence.

INTRODUCTION

As a Level 1 beauty therapist it is a requirement that you support your colleagues by providing assistance with services delivered to clients. One of your roles is to prepare and maintain the working areas for the following beauty therapy treatments:

- waxing
- eye treatments
- make-up
- manicure
- pedicure
- facial.

Preparing and maintaing the beauty therapy area includes:

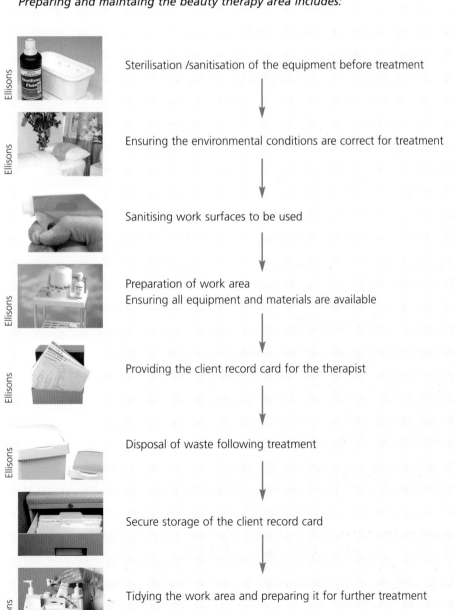

Sterilisation /sanitisation of the equipment before treatment

Ensuring the environmental conditions are correct for treatment

Sanitising work surfaces to be used

Preparation of work area
Ensuring all equipment and materials are available

Providing the client record card for the therapist

Disposal of waste following treatment

Secure storage of the client record card

Tidying the work area and preparing it for further treatment

RECEPTION

You need to allow sufficient time to prepare the work area for each treatment. Check the appointment book schedule regularly to see what treatment is next.

Allow at least 10 minutes to make sure you have all the equipment, materials and products necessary for the treatment. Certain pieces of equipment might have preparation requirements. For example, wax must be heated before use. Allow sufficient time for this, so that the equipment is available for use.

It is important to know how long each treatment service takes so that you are available to tidy the treatment area when it has finished.

Treatment service timings

Treatment service	Length of treatment
Waxing:	
eyebrow wax	15 minutes
underarm wax	15 minutes
half leg wax minutes	30 minutes
bikini line wax	15 minutes
arm wax	30 minutes
full leg	50 minutes
Eye treatments:	
eyebrow shape	15 minutes
eyelash tint	20 minutes
eyebrow tint	10 minutes
eyelash perming	45 minutes
false lashes	20 minutes
Make-up	45 minutes
Manicure	45 minutes
Pedicure	45 minutes
Facial	60 minutes

A description of each treatment service follows, with explanations of how to prepare and maintain each treatment working area. For each service it is important that hygienic practice is considered before preparing the beauty therapy work area and during its maintenance. This will help prevent cross-infection – the transfer of harmful bacteria/micro-organisms from one person to another.

Depending on the equipment required for each beauty therapy service, they can be prepared hygienically either by sanitation or by sterilisation methods:

- **Sterilisation** destroys all living micro-organisms
- Sanitisation destroys some, but not all, micro-organisms.

An autoclave is used when small pieces of equipment need to be sterilised. This heats water to a temperature of 121–134°C. Metal objects and some sponge materials can be sterilised in an autoclave.

Sanitisation is achieved by placing small pieces equipment – often plastic, which is unsuitable for the high temperatures achieved in the autoclave – in a chemical disinfectant or in an ultraviolet cabinet.

Hygiene checks

- Ensure that all tools and equipment are clean and sterile before use.
- Disinfect work surfaces regularly.
- Use disposable items whenever possible.
- Follow hygienic practices.
- Maintain a high standard of personal hygiene.

An autoclave

An ultraviolet light cabinet

PREPARING AND MAINTAINING THE BEAUTY THERAPY WORK AREA FOR WAXING

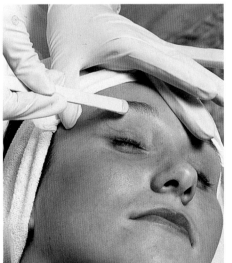

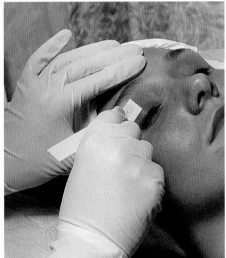

Waxing the eyebrow

Wax treatment involves using wax to remove hairs temporarily from the face and body. Waxing removes both the visible hair and the root, so the re-growth is completely new, soft, fine hairs. It will be 4–6 weeks before the client requires the service again.

Ellisons

Honey wax

Salon Systems

Hot wax discs

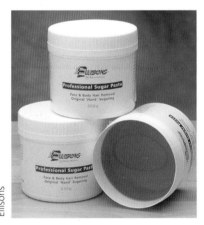

Ellisons

Sugar paste

Ellisons

Strip sugar

Pretreatment

Equipment and materials

There are different wax formulations and systems available for use. Your salon might use only one, or more than one system. Select and prepare the choice of wax as guided by the beauty therapist who will be performing the treatment:

- Warm wax is heated in a special, low-temperature heater to around 43°C, when it becomes runny. Warm waxes are frequently made of mixtures of glucose syrup or honey, and zinc oxide.

- Hot wax is applied at a higher temperature than warm wax – around 50°C. Blocks or pellets of solid wax are heated in a special heater until a thickish, runny consistency is achieved.

- Sugaring is an ancient and popular method of hair removal. A mixture of sugar, lemon and water is applied as a paste, called **sugar paste**, or as a traditional warm wax called **strip sugar**.

- The roller system uses warm wax contained in cartridges, which are heated to the correct working temperature. A disposable applicator head is provided for each client.

Refer to the equipment and materials checklist opposite to make sure you have everything that is needed for the waxing treatment.

Sterilisation and sanitisation

- Small metal tools should be sterilised after use. Clean them with surgical spirit and clean cotton wool and then sterilise them in the autoclave. They should be stored in the ultraviolet cabinet after sterilisation to keep them sanitised and ready for use.
- Towels should be boil washed to destroy harmful micro-organisms and prevent cross-infection.
- Wash your hands before handling clean equipment.

HEALTH AND SAFETY

Personal Protective Equipment (PPE) at Work Regulations (1992)
As there is a risk of contact with body fluids during waxing, it is recommended that special protective equipment is worn. This includes surgical gloves.
It is the employer's responsibility to make these available to employees; it is the employee's responsibility to wear them.

HEALTH AND SAFETY

Prevent cross-infection
If you have a cut on your hand you should wear a protective sterile dressing to prevent cross-infection.

EQUIPMENT AND MATERIALS CHECKLIST

	Warm wax	Hot wax	Roller wax	Strip sugar	Sugar paste
Couch – with sit-up and lie-down positions and an easy-to-clean surface	☐	☐	☐	☐	☐
Trolley – to hold all the necessary equipment and materials	☐	☐	☐	☐	☐
Protective plastic couch cover	☐	☐	☐	☐	☐
Disposable tissue roll	☐	☐	☐	☐	☐
Disposable wooden spatulas – a selection of different sizes used for different body parts	☐	☐		☐	
Wax removal strips (bonded fibre) cut to size for the waxing service	☐	☐	☐	☐	
Talcum powder (purified) to prevent the wax from sticking to the skin		☐			☐
Cotton wool pads, to cleanse and apply products to the skin	☐	☐	☐	☐	☐
Facial tissues, to protect client's clothing and to blot the skin dry	☐	☐	☐	☐	☐
Skin cleanser (pre-wax lotion) to remove surface dirt, cosmetic products, dead skin and body oils	☐	☐	☐	☐	☐
Surgical spirit or a commercial cleaner designed to clean equipment	☐	☐	☐	☐	☐
Towels for protecting the client's clothing and for modesty when clothing has been removed	☐	☐	☐	☐	☐
Small scissors for trimming long hairs before waxing	☐	☐	☐	☐	
A jar of sanitising solution to hold small metal tools, i.e. scissors	☐	☐	☐	☐	☐
Tweezers for removing stray hairs	☐	☐	☐	☐	☐
Wax Select according to organisations/ therapists preferred system					
Afterwax lotion with soothing, healing and cooling properties, to be applied after hair removal	☐	☐	☐	☐	☐
Mirror (clean) – for facial waxing	☐	☐	☐	☐	☐
Apron – to protect workwear from wax spillages	☐	☐	☐	☐	☐
Disposable surgical gloves – used when waxing the underarm and bikini areas.	☐	☐	☐	☐	☐
Bin (swing top) – lined with a disposable bin liner	☐	☐	☐	☐	☐
Client record card – to record clients personal details before and after treatment	☐	☐	☐	☐	☐
Aftercare leaflets – to provide guidance notes for the client to follow after treatment	☐	☐	☐	☐	☐

Sorisa

Sorisa

Ellisons

Ellisons

Sorisa

Ellisons

Ellisons

Ellisons

Ellisons

PhD
waxing system

Preparing the treatment area

1 The area should be clean and tidy.

2 Check the temperature of the working area, the client must not be too warm or she will perspire, which will affect adherence of the wax to the skin. Increase ventilation in the treatment area as necessary.

3 There should be a clean, empty bin in the treatment area, lined with a bin liner.

4 Disinfect all work surfaces and cover them with clean, disposable paper tissue.

5 Check the trolley to make sure it contains everything that is needed to carry out the treatment.

6 Collect metal tools i.e. scissors and tweezers from the ultraviolet cabinet and put them in a sanitising solution on the trolley.

7 The wax must be at a suitable temperature for use: heated as recommended by the manufacturer according to wax type:

- **warm wax** is heated in a heater or cartridge to between 43 and 48°C – when it should be warm and fluid in consistency
- **hot wax** is heated to 50°C
- **strip sugar** wax is heated to 43–48°C
- **sugar paste** is heated in the microwave or heater, following the manufacturer's guidelines, until it is soft
- an individual cartridge of **roller wax** is heated on a medium setting in a heating and storage compartment until it reaches a fluid consistency.

8 The couch should be covered with a clean plastic protective sheet. Disposable paper-tissue bedroll should be placed over the plastic sheet for additional protection and comfort.

9 Place a towel neatly on the couch to protect the client's clothing and to cover her when she has undressed.

10 Position the couch according to the treatment part to be treated. The couch should be in the sit-up position, unless the client is only having her bikini line or under arm areas waxed, in which case it should be flat.

11 Collect the client's record card and place on the treatment trolley.

Post treatment

Disposing of waste products

- Dispose of all wax after use.
- If the roller wax system has been used, replace the disposable applicator with a new one, ready for the next client.
- Clean the wax heaters using equipment cleaner, if there are any wax spillages.
- Dispose of the paper-tissue bedroll.

- Wipe the plastic couch cover with surgical spirit and clean cotton wool to remove any wax spillages.
- Empty the bin that was used to collect waste in the treatment area. Replace the bin liner with a new one.
- Remove used metal tools from the treatment area so that can be sterilised.
- Disposable waste from waxing might have body fluids on it; potentially it is a health risk. It must be handled, collected and disposed of according to the local environmental health regulations. It is a good idea to wear disposable protective gloves when cleaning up and disposing of waste products and materials after treatment; they will help protect you from contact with body fluids.

HEALTH AND SAFETY

Contaminated waste
A yellow sharps container should be available for waste contaminated with blood or tissue fluids.

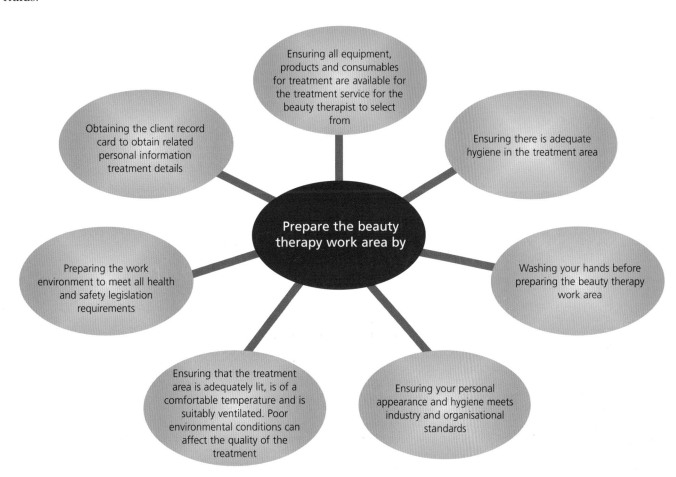

Other post treatment actions

- Check the wax level in the different wax heaters regularly, and replenish with new wax as necessary. This should be done in advance of the next treatment application so that the wax is at the correct temperature and working consistency.
- Protective towels should be removed from the treatment area and should be laundered.
- Return the client record card to the secure storage area for client data.
- At the end of the working day, switch off the wax heater if this system has been used.

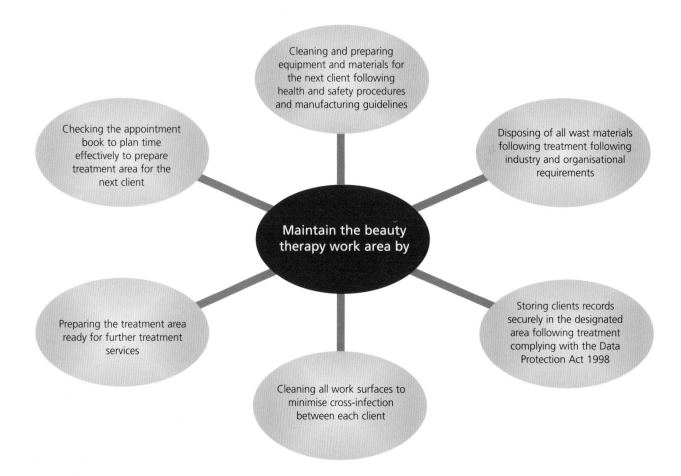

Maintain the beauty therapy work area by

Cleaning and preparing equipment and materials for the next client following health and safety procedures and manufacturing guidelines

Disposing of all wast materials following treatment following industry and organisational requirements

Storing clients records securely in the designated area following treatment complying with the Data Protection Act 1998

Cleaning all work surfaces to minimise cross-infection between each client

Preparing the treatment area ready for further treatment services

Checking the appointment book to plan time effectively to prepare treatment area for the next client

PREPARING AND MAINTAINING THE BEAUTY THERAPY WORK AREA FOR EYE TREATMENTS

Eye treatment involves preparation for any of the following treatments:

- eye brow shaping
- eyelash and eyebrow permanent tinting
- false lash application, either strip lashes or individual lashes
- eyelash perming.

Eyebrow shaping

Eyebrow shaping treatment involves removing the brow hair, to maintain a shape or create a new shape. Hairs are removed using small metal tools called tweezers. There are two types – manual and automatic:

- manual tweezers remove stray hairs and are used to accentuate the brow shape
- automatic tweezers (as shown in the photos of tweezing below) are designed to remove the bulk of excess hair, they have a spring-loaded action.

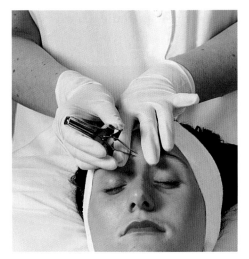

Tweezing at the bridge of the nose with automatic tweezers

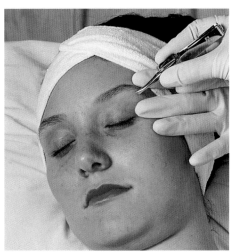

Tweezing at the outer corner of the eyebrow

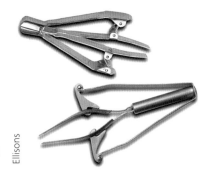

Ellisons

Automatic tweezers

TIP	
Brow hairs Brow hairs can be removed quickly using wax, which is basically mass tweezing.	

Ellisons

Manual tweezers

Eyelash and eyebrow tinting

The hairs of the eyelashes and brows are permanently coloured using a dye to enhance the appearance of the eye area. The tinting treatment can be performed on the eyelashes, the eyebrow area or to both.

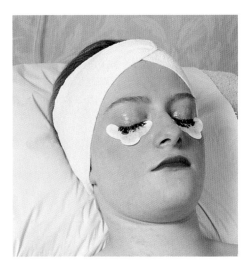

Processing the eyelash tint

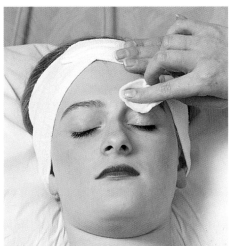

Removing the eyebrow tint from the first eyebrow

Ellisons

Coloured permanent tints, available in black, brown, blue and grey ☐

Hydrogen peroxide – 10 vol, 3% strength ☐

Petroleum jelly, to protect the skin from staining ☐

Ellisons

Eye shields to protect from staining or chemical irritation ☐ ☐

Non-metallic bowl to mix the permanent tint and hydrogen peroxide ☐

Ellisons

Disposable brushes to apply the permanent tint ☐

Surgical spirit to wipe the points of the tweezers to remove artificial eyelash adhesive ☐

Ellisons

Eyelash adhesive for strip lashes. Eyelash adhesive for individual lashes ☐

Strip eyelash lengths a selection of colours and lengths Individual lashes a selection of colours and lengths ☐

Ellisons

Eyelash adhesive solvent for the removal of individual false lashes ☐

Scissors to trim the length of the strip lash ☐

Ellisons

Sterilised small dish lined with foil to place the eyelash adhesive in during lash application ☐

Mild eyelash perm solution to curl the hair ☐

Fixing lotion to make the new eyelash curl permanent ☐

Ellisons

Eyelash curler – a selection of different sizes to curl the natural lashes around during the curling process ☐

Eyelash adhesive to secure short lashes to the eyelash curler ☐

Sonisa

Lint-free pad to remove the perm and fixing lotion ☐

Disposable cocktail sticks to fix the hairs into the correct position around the eyelash curler ☐

Ellisons

Disposable brushes or cotton buds to apply the perm lotion and fixing lotion ☐

Hand mirror (clean) to show the client the results ☐ ☐ ☐ ☐

Bin (swing-top) lined with a disposable bin liner ☐ ☐ ☐ ☐

Client's record card so that the client's details can be recorded before and after treatment ☐ ☐ ☐ ☐

Sterilisation and sanitisation

- Small metal tools should be sterilised after use. Clean them with surgical spirit and clean cotton wool and then sterilise them in the autoclave. Store them in the ultraviolet cabinet after sterilisation, ready for use.
- Applicators for permanent tinting and eyelash perming should be disposable, and thrown away after use.
- Towels should be boil washed to destroy harmful micro-organisms and prevent cross-infection.
- Wash your hands before handling clean equipment.

TIP

Sterilized tweezers
Always have more than one pair of sterilised tweezers available. A clean, sterile pair will be required if the beauty therapist drops the tweezers being used on the floor.

Preparing the treatment area

1 The area should be clean and tidy.

2 There should be a clean, empty bin in the treatment area lined with a bin liner.

3 Disinfect all work surfaces and cover with clean, disposable, paper tissue.

4 Check the trolley to make sure it contains everything that will be needed to carry out the treatment.

5 Collect metal tools from the ultraviolet cabinet, put them into a disinfectant solution and place them on the trolley.

6 Prepare cotton wool: provide a selection of damp and dry cotton wool on the trolley, usually in small bowls.

7 Display the materials and products required for the eye treatment.

8 The beauty couch or chair should be protected with a long strip of disposable bedroll or a freshly laundered sheet and bath towel.

9 For eye treatments the treatment couch should be slightly elevated, not flat.

10 A small towel should be placed neatly at the head of the couch – this will be draped across the client's chest for hygiene and protection during the treatment. The bedroll or sheet will need to be changed, and freshly laundered towels replaced, before the next client.

11 Collect the client's record card and put it on the treatment trolley.

HEALTH AND SAFETY

Storing chemicals
Do not put chemicals such as eyelash perm lotion near to a wax heater on the trolley. The heat could affect the quality (and performance) of the chemicals and they could even become dangerous if they are flammable.
Make sure you follow the COSHH (Control of Substances Hazardous to Health) guidelines on how equipment should be stored (see Chapter 1).

Post treatment

- Dispose of the paper-tissue bedroll.
- Empty the bin that was used to collect waste in the treatment area. Replace the bin liner with a new one.
- Clean small bowls used to hold cotton wool in warm, soapy water; rinse the bowls and dry.
- It is a good idea to wear disposable protective gloves when cleaning up and

Post treatment

- Dispose of the paper-tissue bedroll.
- The bin to collect waste in the treatment areas should be emptied. Replace the bin liner with a new one.
- Clean small bowls in warm, soapy water; rinse and dry.
- Clean the make-up brushes and make-up sponges in warm water and detergent; rinse thoroughly in clean water and allow them to dry naturally. Once dry, place in the ultraviolet cabinet. An alcohol-based cleaner can be used to clean brushes. The brushes are first cleaned as above. When dry they are briefly immersed in the alcohol solution and are then allowed to dry before placing in the ultraviolet cabinet.
- Clean the make-up palette in warm water and detergent, it might be necessary to remove stubborn marks with surgical spirit and clean cotton wool. Place in the ultraviolet cabinet.
- Ensure that the make-up products are clean, use a damp piece of cotton wool and surgical spirit to clean palettes and containers.
- Protective towels and head-band, if used, should be removed from the treatment area and laundered.
- Return the client record card to the secure storage area for client data.

HEALTH AND SAFETY	✚

Laundry
Dirty laundry should be placed in a covered container until cleaned.

PREPARING AND MAINTAINING THE BEAUTY THERAPY WORK AREA FOR MANICURE OR PEDICURE TREATMENT

Manicure and pedicures are treatments applied to the hands and feet:

- Manicure is a treatment to improve the appearance and condition of the hands, nails and skin

- Pedicure is a treatment to improve the appearance and condition of the feet, nail and skin.

In addition to the manicure, specialist therapeutic treatments may be applied. These include:

- Paraffin wax treatment, a heat therapy treatment in which the hand or foot has heated liquid paraffin wax. This creates a heat-maintaining barrier for the skin. It takes approximately 20 minutes for the wax to melt to the correct consistency.

- Thermal booties, insulated boots for the feet are electrically heated to aid the absorption of treatment products from the skin of the feet.

- Thermal mitts, insulated gloves for the hands are electrically heated to aid the absorption of treatment products from the skin of the hands.

- Exfoliator cream can be applied to remove dead skin and soften the skin. The skin appears brighter after treatment.

- Treatment masks, selected to stimulate, rejuvinate or nourish the skin. The hands can be placed in thermal mitts to intensify the effects achieved.

- Warm oil, oil is gently heated and applied to soften the skin and cuticles.

A client receiving a manicure

A client receiving a pedicure

Thermal booties

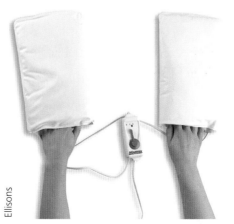

Thermal mitts

Warm oil heater

Pretreatment

Refer to the equipment and materials checklist to make sure that you have all that is required for manicure or pedicure treatment.

EQUIPMENT AND MATERIALS CHECKLIST

	MANICURE	PEDICURE
Manicure/Pedicure table or trolley	☐	☐
Medium-sized towels: three for manicure, five for pedicure	☐	☐
Small bowls lined with tissues (3) for clean cotton wool	☐	☐
Dry cotton wool to apply and remove products	☐	☐
Finger bowl for the client's fingers – to cleanse and soften the skin in warm water	☐	☐
Foot bowl or spa for the client's feet – to cleanse and soften the skin in warm water		☐
Emery board to file the nails to shape	☐	☐
Orange sticks, tipped at either end to with cotton wool, to apply products to the nails and to clean the nail	☐	☐
Cuticle knife to remove skin from the nail	☐	☐
Hoof stick to push back the skin (the cuticle) around the bottom of the nail	☐	☐
Cuticle nippers to remove and neaten the appearance of excess cuticle	☐	☐
Nails scissors used to reduce the length of the nails	☐	☐
Toenail clippers to shorten the length of the toenails	☐	☐
Buffers to give the nail a sheen and to increase blood circulation to the nail	☐	
Buffing paste, a coarse gritty nail product used to shine the nail plate when used with the buffer.	☐	
Detergent, to add to the warm water in the finger bowl or foot spa to cleanse and refresh the skin	☐	☐
Callus file to remove excess skin from the feet		☐
Hand cream, oil or lotion to soften and nourish the skin	☐	

Ellisons
Ellisons
Ellisons
Ellisons
Ellisons

Salon Systems
hand defence
AGE DEFYING HAND CREAM
PROTECTS & NOURISHES

Sonisa

	Manicure	Pedicure
Foot cream, oil or lotion to soften and nourish the skin		☐
Skin sanitiser to cleanse the skin before treatment	☐	☐
Base coat polish to provide a base to apply coloured polish and to prevent nail staining	☐	☐
Coloured polishes, a selection	☐	☐
Top coat to seal and protect nail polish colour providing durability	☐	☐
Specialist nail treatment products such as nail strengthener	☐	☐
Nail polish remover, to remove nail polish from the nail	☐	☐
Cuticle remover to soften the skin of the cuticle and to aid its removal	☐	☐
Cuticle oil to soften and nourish the skin of the cuticle	☐	☐
Cuticle massage cream to soften and nourish the skin of the cuticle	☐	☐
Jar of sanitising solution to hold small metal and plastic manicure tools	☐	☐
Paraffin wax treatment, specialist skin and nail treatment	☐	☐
Thermal booties, specialist skin and nail treatment		☐
Thermal mitts, specialist skin and nail treatment	☐	
Exfoliator cream to remove dead skin cells from the treatment area	☐	☐
Treatment masks, specialist skin treatment	☐	☐
Warm oil treatment, specialist skin and nail treatment	☐	
Plastic bags or plastic film to wrap the hands after the application of a heat or treatment mask	☐	☐
Bin (swing-top) – lined with a disposable bin liner	☐	☐
Client's record card – to record the client's details before and after treatment	☐	☐
Aftercare leaflets might be provided to the client on how to care for the nails	☐	☐

Ellisons
Salon Systems
Ellisons
Salon Systems
Salon Systems
Ellisons
Ellisons
Salon Systems
Ellisons

Sterilisation and sanitisation

- Ensure tools and equipment are clean and sterile before use.
- Small metal tools should be sterilised after use. Clean them with surgical spirit and clean cotton wool and then sterilise them in the autoclave.
- Several sets of manicure/pedicure tools are required to ensure that time is allowed for sanitisation/sterilisation after each treatment.
- Towels should be boil washed to destroy harmful micro-organisms and prevent cross-infection.
- Wash your hands before handling clean equipment.

Preparing the treatment area

1   The area should be clean and tidy.

2   There should be a clean, empty bin in the treatment area lined with a bin liner.

3   Disinfect all work surfaces and cover with clean disposable paper tissue.

4   Check the trolley to make sure it has everything necessary to carry out the treatment.

5   Check whether a heat therapy treatment is to be applied. If using warm paraffin wax, make sure there is sufficient wax in the heater. Adjust the temperature according to manufacturer's instructions. Warm oil in the heater, following the manufacturer's instructions

6   Collect the small metal/plastic manicure/pedicure tools from the ultraviolet cabinet and place them in the jar of sanitising solution.

7   Put all materials neatly onto the trolley.

8   A small table light might be needed for additional light when performing manicure treatment.

9   For **manicure**, place a towel over the work surface, then fold another towel into a pad and place it in the middle of the work surface. The pad supports the client's forearm during treatment. Place a third towel over the pad. Position a chair on either side of the manicure station, one for the client the other for the beauty therapist. Fill the finger bowl with warm water and detergent. Place a tissue or disposable manicure mat on top of the towels.

10   For **pedicure**, place a towel on the floor in between the therapist and client. Fill the foot bowl with warm water and detergent and put it on this towel. Five towels are required: one for the beauty therapist to place on her lap for protection, another should be provided to dry the client's feet, the other two are used to wrap the client's feet to keep warm during pedicure treatment.

11   Collect the client's record card and put it on the treatment trolley.

HEALTH AND SAFETY

Use of electrical equipment
Place equipment on a stable trolley and make sure that the wires do not trail or are in such a position that they might cause an accident.

Post treatment

- Dispose of the paper-tissue bedroll and other disposable items such as emery boards, spatulas and orange sticks.
- Empty the bin that was used to collect waste in the treatment area. Replace the bin liner with a new one.
- Clean small bowls in warm, soapy water; rinse and dry.
- Clean all tools and metal equipment with surgical spirit and sterilise in the autoclave.
- Plastic equipment should be cleaned in warm soapy water, dried and placed in the ultraviolet cabinet.
- Dispose of the brushes used to apply paraffin wax; they cannot be cleaned.
- The buffer, if used, should have the chamois leather cover cleaned in warm soapy water at 60°C. When dried, it should be sanitised in the ultraviolet cabinet. The plastic handle should be wiped with surgical spirit.
- Clean mask brushes in warm, soapy water, dry and put in the ultraviolet cabinet.
- Electrical equipment should be cleaned to remove any spillage. Switch off equipment before cleaning and use specialist equipment cleaner to clean. If the equipment is to be used again, switch on after cleaning. Replenish products as necessary.
- Clean the necks of bottles and jars to maintain hygiene and a high standard of presentation. Nail polish bottle necks should be cleaned regularly with clean cotton wool and nail polish remover to ensure that they close tightly or the polish will become thick in consistency.
- Disinfect work surfaces.
- Remove used towels from the treatment area and launder them.
- Return the client record card to the secure storage area for client data.

PREPARING AND MAINTAINING THE BEAUTY THERAPY WORK AREA FOR FACIAL TREATMENT

A facial is a treatment applied to the skin of the face that has a cleansing, toning, nourishing effect of the skin.

A client receiving a facial treatment

Pretreatment

Refer to the equipment and materials checklist to make sure that you have all that is required for facial treatment.

EQUIPMENT AND MATERIALS CHECKLIST

Sonisa

Couch or beauty chair with sit-up and lie-down positions and an easy-to-clean surface ☐

Trolley to hold the necessary equipment and materials ☐

Sonisa

Large and medium-sized towels to protect the client's clothing and for the beauty therapist to dry her hands during treatment
Note: The client could be offered a gown to wear, place a clean gown in the treatment area. ☐

Ellisons

Disposable tissue such as bedroll ☐

Ellisons

Head-band to protect the client's hair and to keep hair away from the treatment area ☐

Dampened, clean cotton wool, to remove skincare products ☐

Ellisons

Cotton wool eye pads preshaped round and dampened to place over the eyes during the mask treatment.
Note: Two further cotton wool eye pads will be required if facial steaming is being carried out to protect the delicate eye tissue. ☐

Ellisons

Facial tissues to blot the skin dry after toner and following mask removal ☐

Small bowls to store damp and dry cotton wool, mix treatment masks, hold cosmetic creams that have been dispensed ☐

Ellisons

Spatulas to remove products hygienically from containers and to tuck the client hair underneath the head-band to prevent soiling. ☐

Ellisons

Non-oily eye make-up remover to cleanse the eye area (to prevent the make-up being a barrier to treatment) ☐

Cleansing lotion – a range available to suit the different skin types Normal, dry, combination, oily, sensitive ☐

Ellisons

Toning lotion – a range available to suit the different skin types Normal, dry, combination, oily, sensitive ☐

Salon Systems

Moisturiser – a range available to suit the different skin types
Normal, dry, combination, oily, sensitive

☐

Salon Systems

Mask brush to apply facial masks

☐

Salon Systems

Massage oil/cream

☐

Magnifier lamp (cold) to enlarge the appearance of the treatment area

☐

Ellisons

Skin warming device:
facial steamer vapour unit
towel steaming

☐
☐

Sorisa

Distilled water to fill the tank of the vapour unit
Note: Consult the beauty therapist to see if she is using a skin warming
device in her treatment.

☐

Skin exfoliation product, to remove the surface dead skin cells
exposing fresh new cells.

☐

Ellisons

Specialist skin products:
eye creams   eye gels
lip balms   neck creams   acne products

☐

Ellisons

Setting masks, which absorb dead skin, the skin's natural oil (sebum)
and debris – usually to cleanse and improve the skin tone.
Note: Some masks require other ingredients to be added. Check
what is required for the mask treatment with the beauty therapist
when preparing the work area.

☐

Ellisons

Non-setting masks containing emollients – skin softening ingredients
that soften and nourish the skin

☐

Ellisons

Mask removal sponges. Large, high-quality cotton wool discs
can be used in preference to sponges.
Note: If a sink is not available for the beauty therapist, a large bowl
will be required filled with warm water to remove the mask.

☐

Ellisons

Mirror (clean) to show the client the skin after treatment

☐

Bin (swing-top) lined with a disposable bin liner

☐

Ellisons

Client record card – to record client's personal details before and
after treatment

☐

Sterilisation and sanitisation

- Ensure tools and equipment are clean and sterile before use.
- Several sets of facial sponges and mask brushes will be required to ensure that time is allowed for sanitisation/sterilisation after each treatment.
- Towels should be boil washed to destroy harmful micro-organisms and prevent cross-infection.
- Wash your hands before handling clean equipment.

Preparing the treatment area

1 The area should be clean and tidy.

2 There should be a clean, empty bin lined with a bin liner.

3 Disinfect all work surfaces and cover with clean disposable paper tissue.

4 Check the trolley to make sure it contains everything needed to carry out the treatment.

5 Collect facial equipment from the ultraviolet cabinet, mask brush and mask removal sponges and place on the trolley.

6 Prepare cotton wool: provide a selection of damp and dry cotton wool placed on the trolley, usually in small bowls.

7 The beauty couch or chair should be protected with a long strip of disposable bedroll or a freshly laundered sheet and bath towel.

8 Adjust the lighting – the room should be gently lit for facial treatment, to induce relaxation.

9 Check that the magnifying lamp is clean and in good working area.

10 Check the room temperature, good ventilation is important – it should not be too warm.

11 A large towel should be should be provided to cover the client's body and a small towel to drape across the client's chest and shoulders. Place these neatly on the treatment couch.

12 A clean gown can be provided, if the client prefers, to wear after removing outer clothing (a requirement if the client is receiving facial massage to the chest and shoulders).

13 If a skin-warming device is to be used, this should be prepared ready for use:

    a Hot towels: clean, sterile towels should be placed in the towel warmer. Follow the manufacturer's guidelines for heating timings.

    b Facial steamer vapour unit: fill the water tank with distilled water up to the maximum level. Switch on the machine at the mains, select the steam facility and heat the water until steam can be seen. Switch off the unit. This will save time as the water will now only need to be reheated.

14 Collect the client's record card and place on the treatment trolley.

Ellisons

A towel warmer

Sonisa

A vapour unit

Post treatment

- Dispose of the paper-tissue bedroll.
- Empty the bin that was used to collect waste in the treatment areas. Replace the bin liner with a new one.
- Disinfect work surfaces.
- Clean bowls used in warm soapy water, rinse and dry.
- Clean the mask brushes in warm water and detergent, rinse thoroughly in clean water and allow them to dry naturally. Once dry, place them in the ultraviolet cabinet.
- Wash the mask-removal sponges in warm water and detergent and then sterilise in the autoclave. Place in the ultraviolet cabinet when dry, ready for use.
- Ensure the facial steamer, if used, is switched off and disconnected at the mains. Check the water level and refilled with distilled water ready for future use.
- Used towels, including facial towels used to warm the skin, the head-band and gown (if worn) should be removed from the treatment area and laundered.
- Return the client record card to the secure storage area for client data.

Glossary

Cross-infection	the transfer of contagious micro-organisms
Data Protection Act (1998)	legislation designed to protect client privacy and confidentiality
Environmental conditions	the surroundings in which the treatment will be performed
Eye-brow-shaping treatment	removal of brow hair to maintain or create a new shape
Eye-lash-perming treatment	the use of chemical lotions to permanently curl the lash hair
Eye treatments	treatments applied to the eye area to enhance the appearance of the eye
Eyelash and eyebrow treatment treatment	the permanent colouring of the lash and/or brow hair using a specialist dye to enhance their appearance
Facial	a treatment applied to the skin of the face; it has a skin cleansing, toning and nourishing effect
False lash treatment	threads of artificial hair attached to the natural lashes to make them appear thicker and longer
Hygiene	the recommended standard of cleanliness necessary in the salon to prevent cross-infection

Glossary

Legislation	laws that affect the beauty therapy business and which relate to products and services, the business premises and environmental conditions, working practises and those employed
Maintain	to keep
Make-up treatment	the application of make-up cosmetics to enhance the skin and facial features
Manicure treatment	a treatment to improve the appearance of the hands, nails and skins
Pedicure treatment	a treatment to improve the appearance of the feet, nails and skins
Personal Protective Equipment (PPE) at Work Regs (1992)	legislation that requires employers to identify, through risk assessment, those activities that require special protective equipment to be worn
Preparation	to get ready
Record card	personal information recorded for each client, also recording treatments received and retail products purchases
Sanitisation	the destruction of some but not all micro-organisms
Sterilisation	the destruction of all micro-organisms
Waxing	the use of wax to remove hairs temporarily from the face and body

Assessment and knowledge of understanding

Unit BT1: Prepare and maintain the beauty therapy work area

You have now learned how to prepare and maintain the beauty therapy work area for waxing, eye treatments, manicure, pedicure and facial treatments. The skills developed enable you to professionally prepare and maintain the beauty therapy work area. To test your level of knowledge and understanding, answer the following short questions, these will prepare you for your summative (final) assessment.

Preparing the beauty therapy work area:

1 Why is it important to keep accurate client records?

2 Why is it important that you wash your hands before preparing the work area?

3 Why is it important to follow the senior therapist's instructions for preparing the work area?

4 How can cross-infection be avoided when preparing the work area?

5 How can you ensure your own personal hygiene? Give three examples.

6 Define the terms:
   a sterilisation
   b sanitisation

7 Name a piece of equipment used to sterilise objects.

8 Name a piece of equipment used to sanitise objects.

9 What chemicals are used for sanitising objects?

10 Why must you check the environmental conditions when preparing the work area: heating, lighting and ventilation?

Maintaining the beauty therapy work area:

1 How should wax waste be disposed of?

2 Why should the manufacturer's instructions be followed when using treatment materials and equipment?

3 Why should you know the storage requirements for different products?

4 Why should you regularly check the appointment book when planning your time to prepare and maintain the work areas for different treatments?

5 Where should the client's records be stored after treatment?

6 How should you aim to leave the treatment area after treatment?

7 How would you clean the following:
   a metal manicure tools
   b make-up brushes
   c wax heater
   d eyelash tinting bowls
   e facial mask brush and sponges

chapter 4

ASSIST WITH FACIAL TREATMENTS

Learning objectives

This chapter covers the skills and knowledge you need to assist with facial treatments. It describes the competencies to enable you to:

- prepare for facial treatments

- carry out facial treatments

- complete the treatments.

When performing facial treatments, it is important to consider health and safety at all times using the knowledge you have learnt in Unit G1 Ensure your own actions reduce risks to health and safety (see Chapter 1).

		✓
1	The treatment aim of a basic facial treatment	
2	Contra-indications that prevent a facial treatment	
3	Equipment and products needed	
4	Preparing the treatment area	
5	Preparing yourself before the facial treatment	
6	Client consultation and preparing the client	
7	How to carry out the basic facial treatment	
8	After-care and advice for the client	
9	Contra-actions to the facial treatment	

When you have ticked all the areas you can ask your assessor to assess you on
Unit BT2: Assist with facial treatments. After practical assessment, your assessor
might decide that you need to practice further to improve your skills. If so,
your assessor will tell you how and where you need to improve to gain
competence.

INTRODUCTION

As well as looking after the skin from the inside, by diet, it needs care from the
outside – it must be kept clean and it must be nourished.

When it is functioning normally, the skin becomes greasy and sweat is
deposited on its surface. The natural oil in the skin (called sebum) can easily
build up on the skin's surface and block the natural openings – the pores – on
the surface of the skin; this can lead to infection. Facial cosmetics also affect
the health of the skin; if not regularly removed, they can cause blockages. Skin-
care treatments help to maintain and improve the functioning of the skin.

The basic facial treatment aims to improve the appearance and condition of
the skin by the application of appropriate cosmetic treatments and
preparations. The facial treatment includes:

- consultation and skin analysis
- skin cleansing
- skin toning
- the application of a face mask
- moisturiser application.

The skin varies in appearance, according to our race, sex and age. It alters from season to season, year to year and reflects our general health, lifestyle and diet. The functioning of the different parts of the skin gives us our **skin type**, e.g. dry, oily or combination.

You need to know about the skin, its structure and function so that you can improve its appearance and understand how to care for it properly.

THE ANATOMY AND PHYSIOLOGY OF THE SKIN

Basic functions of the skin

Protection

The skin helps to protect the body from harmful substances and conditions, and cushions the underlying structures in the body from physical injury. The outer surface of the skin is bactericidal, which helps to prevent the growth of harmful micro-organisms. The tough, waterproof construction of the skin forms a barrier that prevents the absorption of many substances, and also prevents the skin losing vital water, which would cause it to dry out. Cells in the skin contain a pigment called melanin, which gives us our skin colour and absorbs harmful rays of ultraviolet light. The amount of melanin in the skin varies between individuals and between races.

Temperature control

Body temperature is controlled in part by heat loss through the skin and by sweating.

Sensitivity

The skin allows the feelings of **touch**, **pressure**, **heat** and **cold**, and allows us to recognise objects by their feel and shape.

HEALTH AND SAFETY

Allergic reactions
If the skin is allergic or is sensitive to a substance this shows as an **allergic** reaction. The skin becomes red itchy and swollen. At the consultation you must check whether a client is allergic to anything so that you don't cause an allergic reaction.

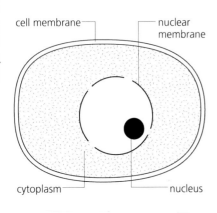

cell membrane — ⌐ nuclear membrane

cytoplasm — nucleus

A cell

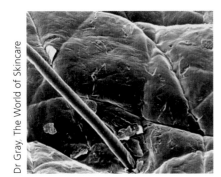

The outer layer of the skin's epidermis shown with an electric microscope

Basic structure of the skin

The skin is the largest organ in the body, accounting for one-eighth of the body's total weight. It is made up of microscopic cells, which provide a tough, flexible covering, and have many important functions. Each cell contains various specialised structures surrounded by a chemical substance called **protoplasm**. The activities of these cells are essential for our general health. If the cells cannot function properly, a disorder results.

Each cell is surrounded by the **cell membrane**. This membrane is porous, allowing food to enter and waste materials to leave.

In the centre of the cell is the **nucleus**, which contains the **chromosomes** that carry the genes we have inherited from our parents. Genes are responsible for cell reproduction and functioning.

The liquid that surrounds the nucleus is called the cell **cytoplasm**.

If we used a microscope to look inside the skin we would be able to see two distinct layers: the **epidermis** (the top layer of the skin) and the **dermis**. Situated below the epidermis and the dermis is a further layer, the **subcutaneous layer** or **fat layer**.

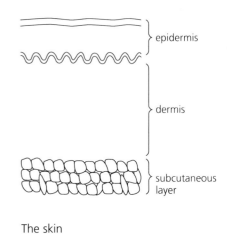

epidermis

dermis

subcutaneous layer

The skin

The epidermis

The main function of the epidermis is to protect the deeper living structures in the body from invasion and harm by the external environment.

The epidermis lies directly above the dermis layer. It is composed of five layers, with the outer surface layer being the skin we can see and touch. This is the most significant layer of the skin with regard to the external application of skin care products. Each layer of the epidermis can be recognised by the shape of its cells.

TIP ✔

Keratin
The main type of cell in the epidermis is the **keratinocyte**, which produces a substance called **keratin**. Keratin makes the skin tough and reduces the entry of substances into the skin. Keratin is the main substance that forms hair and nails.

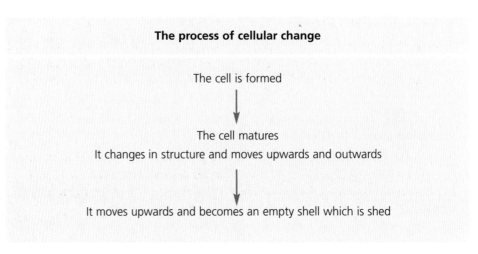

The process of cellular change

The cell is formed
↓
The cell matures
It changes in structure and moves upwards and outwards
↓
It moves upwards and becomes an empty shell which is shed

Over a period of about four weeks, cells move from the bottom layer of the epidermis to the top layer – the skin's surface – changing in shape and structure as they progress through the different layers:

The five layers of the epidermis are:

1 stratum corneum or cornified layer
2 stratum lucidum or clear layer or lucid layer
3 stratum granulosum or granular layer
4 stratum mucosum or spinosum or prickle-cell layer
5 stratum germinativum or basal layer.

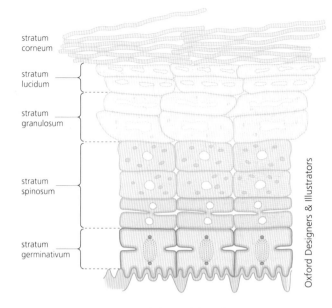
Oxford Designers & Illustrators

Layers of the epidermis

Stratum corneum or cornified layer

This outer layer is formed from several layers of flattened, scale-like overlapping cells, composed mainly of keratin. These help to reflect ultraviolet light from the skin's surface; darker skins can tolerate strong ultraviolet light and has a thicker stratum corneum than paler skins.

It takes about four weeks for the epidermal cells to reach the stratum corneum form the stratum germinativum. The cells are then shed in a process called, **desquamation**.

Stratum lucidum or clear layer or lucid layer

This layer is seen only in non-hairy areas of the skin such as the palms of the hands and soles of the feet. The cells here lack a nucleus and are filled with clear substances called *eledin*.

Stratum granulosum or granular layer

This is composed of two or three layers of flattish cells. The nucleus of the cell has begun to break up, creating granules within the cell cytoplasm. These granules later form keratin.

Stratum mucosum or spinosum or prickle-cell layer

The stratum spinosum or prickle-cell layer is formed from between two and six rows of cells that have a surface of spiky spines, which connect to surrounding cells. Each cell has a large nucleus filled with fluid.

Stratum germinativum or basal layer

This is the deepest layer of the epidermis. It is formed from a single layer of column-shaped cells. These cells divide continuously and produce new cells. Melanocytes are found in this layer; these cells produce the skin pigment melanin and give the skin its colour.

TIP

Removing dead cells
When we cleanse the skin and apply specialist skin products, such as a treatment mask, we remove dead cells from the surface of the epidermis.

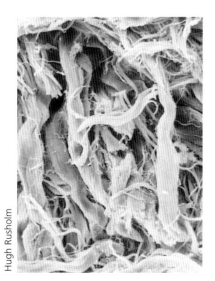
Hugh Rusholm

Collagen and elastin fibres

Dr Gray, The World of Skincare

Aged skin

The dermis

The dermis is the inner part of the skin underneath the epidermis. It is much thicker than the epidermis and contains a network of fibres that give skin its strength and elasticity. There are two types of fibres:

- yellow elastin gives the skin its elasticity
- white collagen gives the skin its strength.

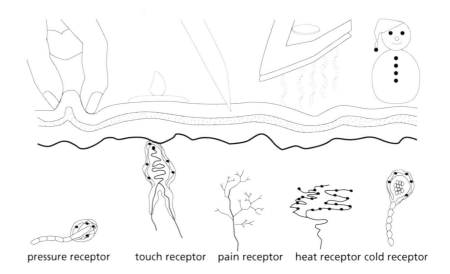

pressure receptor   touch receptor   pain receptor   heat receptor cold receptor

Sensory nerves

As the skin begins to age this network loses strength and elasticity, resulting in facial lines and slack skin.

The dermis also contains different types of nerve ending, which sense touch, pressure and temperature. They inform us about the outside world and what is happening on the skin's surface. They are more numerous in sensitive parts of the skin such as the lips and the fingertips.

Near the surface of the dermis are tiny projections called papillae, these contain nerve endings and blood capillaries. These supply the upper epidermis with nutrition.

The blood supply to the skin

Nutrients and oxygen, which are essential for the skin's health and growth, are brought to the dermis in the blood. The blood vessels that bring blood to the dermis also take away some waste products. Other waste products (e.g. used blood cells) are carried away by the lymph vessels.

TIP ✔

Blood supply
When you massage the skin surface when applying cleansing products you increase the blood supply to the skin and so assist the removal of waste products from the skin. This improves the health and functioning of the skin.

Skin appendages

Within the dermis are structures called skin appendages. These include:

- sweat glands
- hair follicles, which produce hair
- sebaceous glands
- nails.

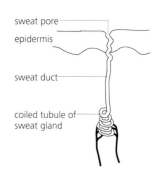

An eccrine sweat gland

Sweat glands

These are small tubes in the skin, extending from the epidermis into the dermis. They are found all over the body, especially on the soles of the feet and palms of the hands. The main function of the sweat glands is to control body temperature. Sweat, a fluid, flows onto the skin surface and evaporates, creating a cooling effect.

Hair follicles

These are downward growths in the epidermis and dermis of the skin. They are found all over the body except on the palms of the hands and soles of the feet. At the bottom of each follicle is a cluster of cells that divide and move up the hair follicle, changing in structure and forming a **hair**.

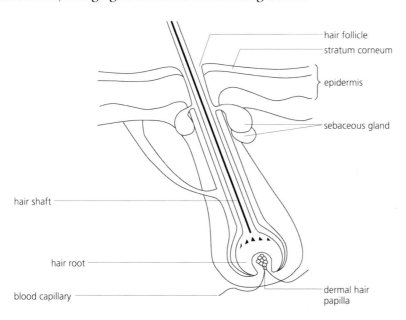

A hair follicle

TIP ✔
Sebum and skin types
An overactive sebaceous gland produces a large amount of sebum and results in an oily skin type.
If the sebaceous gland is underactive, it produces less sebum and the skin is termed dry.

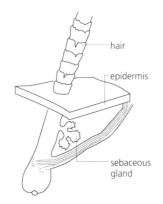

hair

epidermis

sebaceous gland

A sebaceous gland

Sebaceous glands

These are minute sac-like organs. They are found all over the body, except the palms of the hands and soles of the feet. The cells of the gland break down and form an oil called **sebum**. The activity of the sebaceous gland is increased at puberty, when stimulated by a chemical messenger carried in the blood called a hormone. In adults, the activity slows down again. Men secrete slightly more sebum than women.

Sebum has bactericidal and fungicidal properties, which help discourage the growth of harmful micro-organisms on the skin surface, which could lead to skin disease. Sebum also prevents loss of moisture from the surface of the skin.

The acid mantle

Sweat and sebum combine on the skin surface to create an acid film called the acid mantle. This discourages the growth of bacteria and fungi.

HEALTH AND SAFETY ✚

Protecting the skin's acid mantle

Some products that come into contact with the skin (such as some soaps) are alkaline, and can destroy the skin's acid mantle. If these products are used on the skin, the acid mantle will take several hours to restore itself and the skin might become irritated, reddened and sensitive.

SKIN TYPES

The basic skin types that you need to be able to recognise and treat are:

- oily (also known as greasy)
- dry
- combination.

A skin analysis – an inspection of the client's skin – helps us to identify skin type.

How to recognise different skin types

Dr Gray, The World of Skincare

Oily skin

Oily skin

The sebaceous glands are very active, especially at puberty (sexual maturity). An increase in sebum production often causes the appearance of skin blemishes. Sebaceous gland activity begins to decrease in the twenties.

An oily skin:

- has large pores
- has a coarse texture (not smooth)
- appears thick
- is usually sallow (a yellowy colour) as a result of excess sebum production
- appears shiny due to excess sebum production
- possesses good skin strength (tone) because of the protective effect of sebum

- might show certain skin disorders, e.g. comedones (blackheads), pustules and papules (blemishes caused by bacterial infection of the skin).

Dry skin

Dry skin is lacking in sebum, moisture or both. Because sebum limits the loss of moisture from the skin's surface, skin with insufficient sebum loses moisture more quickly becoming **dehydrated**. A dry skin:

- has small tight pores
- has poor moisture content
- has a thin, coarse texture
- often exhibits patches of flaking skin
- often has sensitive areas, showing broken capillaries as a result of reduced sebum protection
- might contain milia (sebaceous blockages, accumulated in the hair follicle) – small, hard, pearly white cysts that are often seen around the eye area.

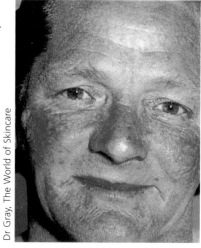

Dr Gray, The World of Skincare

Dry skin

Combination skin

This skin is partly dry and partly oily. The oily parts are generally the chin, nose and forehead known as the **T-zone**. The upper cheeks might also show signs of oiliness but the rest of the face and neck is dry. In a combination skin:

- there are enlarged pores in the T-zone and small to medium-sized pores in the cheek area
- the moisture content is high in the oily areas but poor in the dry area
- the skin is coarse and thick in the oily areas but thinner in the dry areas
- the skin is sallow on the oily areas but shows sensitivity in the dry areas
- the skin tone is good in the oily areas but poor in the dry areas
- there may be blemishes such as pustules and comedones at the T-zone
- milia and broken capillaries might appear in the dry areas, commonly on the cheeks and near the eyes.

Dr Gray, The World of Skincare

Combination skin

Allergic skin

Allergic skin is irritated by external **allergens** – substances that cause sensitivity. The allergens inflame the skin and might damage its protective function. At the consultation, always check whether the client has any allergies, and if so what.

Contact with an allergen, especially if repeated, can cause skin disorders such as eczema and dermatitis. If a skin is sensitive, use hypo-allergenic products those that do not contain any of the known allergens.

FACIAL TREATMENT

A basic facial treatment includes:

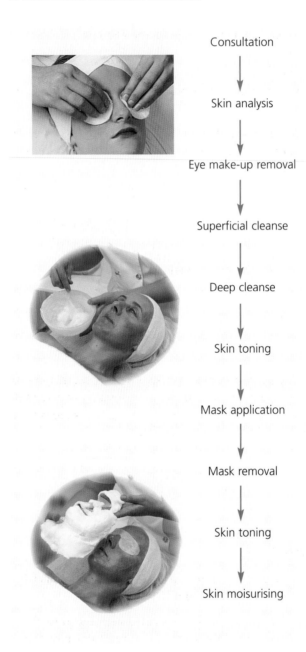

Consultation

↓

Skin analysis

↓

Eye make-up removal

↓

Superficial cleanse

↓

Deep cleanse

↓

Skin toning

↓

Mask application

↓

Mask removal

↓

Skin toning

↓

Skin moisurising

Making the appointment

When a client makes an appointment for a basic facial treatment, the
receptionist should ask a few basic questions:

- What is the client's name and telephone number? This will help you to get
  the client record card ready before they arrive for treatment. The telephone
  number is important in case you need to cancel the treatment for any
  reason, i.e. the beauty therapist is ill.

- Which therapist does the client want to see? If a particular therapist is needed you will have to check on availability.

- When does the client want the treatment, i.e. day/date and time? If any of these are not available, suggest another time or day as near to this as possible.

- Has the client had the treatment before? This allows the client to ask you questions about the treatment.

- Does the client require any other services in addition to the basic facial treatment? Always look at opportunities to increase treatment bookings, the salon needs to keep busy!

Remember, when making an appointment it is important to allow enough time to complete the treatment properly. It is also important for the therapist to be able to complete the treatment in the time allowed.

ACTIVITY	

Timing
What is the time allowed for a basic facial treatment?
Why is it important to complete the treatment in this time?
Think of three reasons for each.

The Data Protection Act (1998)

A client's personal details are confidential, or private. All information relating to a client should be stored securely. Only those staff with permission to access it can do so. Therefore, as soon as all treatment details have been recorded on the record card, the client's details should be stored securely.

Before treatment

Contra-indications to treatment

Certain skin and eye conditions prevent you from performing the basic facial treatment, these are known as **contra-indications**.

If, when looking at the client's skin and eyes before the treatment, you think you recognise any of the following conditions, basic facial treatment must not be carried out. You will need to refer the client tactfully to the relevant person in the salon to get confirmation as to whether the treatment can go ahead.

HEALTH AND SAFETY	

Contra-indication
Remember – you might be wrong when you think you have a client with a contra-indication.
Always check if unsure – the client might be able to have the treatment after all.
Never diagnose and try to avoid causing the client embarrassment.

Conditions that prevent treatment

All the skin and eye conditions listed below are contagious – they can be passed to other clients. You must never treat a client with any of these conditions.

Name of contra-indication	Cause	Appearance
Impetigo 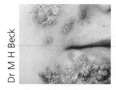 Dr M H Beck	A contagious **bacterial** infection caused by minute, single-celled organisms and which results in skin inflammation	The skin appears red and is itchy. Small blisters appear, which burst and then form crusts
Tiea Corporis or **body ringworm**  Dr M H Beck	A contagious **fungal** infection of the skin. Fungal diseases of the skin feed of the waste products of the skin	Small, scaly red patches spread outwards and then heal from the centre, leaving a ring. Found on the limbs
Conjunctivitis or **pink eye**	A contagious **bacterial** infection of the mucous membrane that covers the eyelids	The skin of the inner conjunctiva of the eye becomes inflamed, the eye becomes very red and sore, and pus might appear
Hordeola or **styes**	A contagious **bacterial** infection of the sebaceous glands of eyelash hair follicles	Small lumps appear, usually containing pus at the skin around the base of the eyelash hair
Furuncles or **boils**  Dr M H Beck	A contagious **bacterial** infection in the skin around the hair follicle	Red, painful lumps extend into the skin around a hair follicle. A core of pus develops
Herpes simplex or **cold sore** 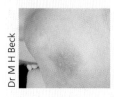 Dr M H Beck	A contagious **viral** disorder of the skin. Viruses require living tissue to survive. They invade the healthy cell and multiply within the cell. Cold sores often appear when skin's resistance is low due to stress or ill health	Inflammation of the skin occurs in localised areas. The skin becomes red and feels itchy, and small blisters appear. These are followed by a crust, which might crack and weep tissue fluid

Conditions that might restrict treatment

The skin conditions below are non-contagious – they cannot be passed to other clients. Clients with these conditions can be treated, but you might need to adapt your treatment application.

Name of contra-indication	Cause	Appearance	Treatment
Skin eczema Dr M H Beck	Inflammation of the skin caused by contact with a skin irritant	The skin becomes red, swells and blisters can appear. The blisters burst, which causes scabs to form on the skin	Ensure you find out what irritants make the eczema worse and avoid contact with such products, e.g. it might be perfumed products. The skin can benefit from cosmetic products that contain soothing ingredients such as lavender. Do not treat if the skin is broken
Skin psoriasis Dr M H Beck	Cause unknown but becomes worse when the person is stressed. Often hereditary	Itchy, red, flaky patches of skin, which can become infected if the skin is broken	The skin can benefit from cosmetic products that contain soothing ingredients such as lavender. Do not treat if the skin is broken
Broken bones	Injury – should be treated medically	The breakage might not be obvious. Therefore, if the client is new, check there have been no recent broken bones at the consultation	The broken bone must not be handled. Always check first with the relevant person in the workplace

---

HEALTH AND SAFETY ✚

Skin disorders
If a client shows a skin disorder and you are at all unsure, check with the relevant person in the workplace before starting treatment.
A client with a skin disorder is usually advised to visit their GP. This is relevant for all contra-indications that prohibit treatment and also for those that restrict treatment mainly eczema and psoraisis.

HEALTH AND SAFETY ✚

Cuts, abrasions, bruising, redness and swelling
If the skin has been damaged but is no longer infected or at risk from secondary infection, you might be able to treat the skin. Check with the senior beauty therapist before you proceed.

Equipment and materials

Refer to the equipment and materials checklist to make sure that you have all that is required to perform a basic facial treatment.

EQUIPMENT AND MATERIALS CHECKLIST

Sorisa

Treatment couch or beauty chair ☐

Sorisa

Equipment trolley on which to place everything required for the facial treatment ☐

Sorisa

Beauty stool; for the comfort of the beauty therapist this should have a back rest and be adjustable in height, to allow mobility ☐

Sorisa

Magnifying lamp (cold) – floor standing or trolley mounted – to enlarge the surface appearance of the skin when performing the skin analysis ☐

Ellisons

Small bowls lined with tissues (3): one for the client's jewellery and two for clean, dry and damp cotton wool ☐

Ellisons

Large bowl to hold warm water during removal of the mask if a sink is not available in the treatment area ☐

Ellisons

Facial skin cleansing preparations to suit all skin types, including eye make-up remover, cleanser, toner and moisturiser ☐

Salon Systems

A skin cleansing preparation that contains a variety of different ingredients to achieve a deep cleansing, toning, nourishing or refreshing effect upon the skin. Select according to skin type ☐

Salon Systems

Mask brush – sanitised for each client – to apply the mask to the skin of the face and neck ☐

Ellisons

Sterilised mask removal sponges (2) for removing the mask in warm water ☐

Head-band ☐

Towels (2) – freshly laundered for each client. A large towel should cover the client's body and a small hand towel should be draped across the client's chest and shoulders ☐

A clean towel for the therapist to use as necessary ☐

A clean gown for each client as necessary ☐

A plentiful supply of damp and dry cotton wool – sufficient for the treatment to be carried out ☐

Cotton buds to cleanse excess make-up left along the lash line following eye cleansing ☐

Facial tissues should be large and of a high quality. They should be stored in a covered container ☐

Hand mirror (clean) for consulting with the client before and after treatment ☐

Several clean spatulas (preferably disposable) for each client. One should be used to tuck any stray hair beneath the head-band; others will be used to remove products from their containers ☐

Covered swing waste bin placed unobtrusively within easy reach. It should be lined with a disposable bin liner ☐

Client's record card to record all personal details and record details of the treatment ☐

Sanitising solution to keep the small tools hygienic once sterilised ☐

BEAUTY WORKS

Date	Therapist name	
Client name		Date of birth (identifying client age group)
Address		Postcode
Evening phone number	Day phone number	
Name of doctor	Doctor's address and phone number	
Related medical history (conditions that may restrict or prohibit treatment application)		
Are you taking any medication (this may affect the appearance of the skin or skin sensitivity)		

CONTRA-INDICATIONS REQUIRING MEDICAL REFERRAL
(Preventing facial treatment application)

- ☐ bacterial infections (e.g. impetigo)
- ☐ viral infections (e.g. herpes simplex)
- ☐ fungal infections (e.g. tinea ungium)
- ☐ eye infections (e.g. conjunctivitis)
- ☐ systemic medical conditions
- ☐ severe skin conditions

SKIN GROUP

☐ oily   ☐ dry   ☐ combination

FACIAL PRODUCTS

- ☐ cleanser
- ☐ toner
- ☐ eye cleanser
- ☐ mask – non-setting
- ☐ moisturiser

CONTRA-INDICATIONS WHICH RESTRICT TREATMENT
(Treatment may require adaption)

- ☐ cuts and abrasions
- ☐ recent scar tissue
- ☐ skin allergies
- ☐ bruising and swelling
- ☐ eczema
- ☐ psoriasis

SKIN CONDITION

- ☐ sensitive
- ☐ dehydrated
- ☐ broken capillaries
- ☐ pustules
- ☐ open pores
- ☐ hypo pigmentation
- ☐ keloids
- ☐ ingrowing hairs

- ☐ mature
- ☐ milia
- ☐ comedones
- ☐ papules
- ☐ hyper pigmentation
- ☐ dermatitis
- ☐ papulosa nigra

EQUIPMENT AND MATERIALS

- ☐ magnifying light
- ☐ spatulas
- ☐ consumables
- ☐ protective covering

Beauty therapist signature (for reference)
Client signature (confirmation of details)

Equipment and products used in a basic facial treatment

Product	Use	Health and safety
Bowls – various sizes	Client jewellery; skin-care preparations; cotton wool; warm water to remove face mask	Clean after use with a detergent, disinfectant, rinse and dry. If using for water, keep on a stable surface to avoid spillage
Skin cleanser	Usually a combination of oil and water that is capable of dissolving grease and other substances from the skins surface. Various cleansing preparations are available to the beauty therapist whose formulations are designed to different skin types	If a client has a sensitive skin use a hypo-allergenic product. Use the correct cleansing product for the skin type to avoid skin irritation or sensitivity. Avoid excessive use of cleanser around the eye are to avoid cleanser entering the eye and causing eye irritation
Skin toner	Applied after the skin has been cleansed. Toning lotions remove all traces of cleanser and skin-care preparations from the skin's surface. They also create a skin-tightening effect, making the pores close. Various toning preparations are available, in formulations for the different skin types	If a client has a sensitive skin use a hypo-allergenic product. Use the correct toning product for the skin type to avoid skin irritation or sensitivity. Replace lids immediately following use to avoid spillage. Gently blot the skin dry following application with a soft facial tissue to avoid stimulating the skin as it evaporates from the skin surface
Eye make-up remover	Eye make-up remover cleanses the eyelids and lashes, gently dissolving make-up if worn. It also conditions the delicate skin. Formulated as a lotion or gel, it is designed to remove either water-based or oil-based products (or both)	If a client has a sensitive skin use a hypo-allergenic product. Support the delicate eye tissue when cleansing the eye to avoid stretching the skin. Avoid excessive use of eye make-up remover as it may enter the eye causing irritation. Never apply pressure over the eyeball when cleansing the eye area
Moisturiser	The skin depends on water to keep it soft and supple. The natural moisture level is constantly being disturbed. The application of a cosmetic moisturiser helps to maintain the natural oil and moisture balance by locking moisture into the skin, offering protection and hydration. The basic formulation of a moisturiser is oil and water	If a client has a sensitive skin use a hypo-allergenic product. Always use a spatula to remove moisturiser if in a container to prevent contamination. Return lids immediately for hygiene and to prevent the quality of the product spoiling
Face mask	A cleansing preparation using a variety of different ingredients to absorb, cleanse, tighten (astringents), soften (emollients) and calm and sooth (desensitisers)	Clean the container following use. Ensure that product is taken from the container using a clean spatula. Never place the mask brush on the client's skin and return to the product or contamination will occur
Mask brush	To apply face mask to the skin of the face and neck. Usually consists of a plastic handle with synthetic bristles	Clean in warm soapy water, allow to dry and store in the ultraviolet cabinet

Sterilisation and sanitisation

It is important that hygienic practice is considered before and throughout the client treatment. This will help prevent cross-infection – the transfer of harmful bacteria/micro-organisms from one person to another.

Hygiene checks

- Ensure that all tools and equipment are clean and sterile before use.
- Disinfect work surfaces regularly.
- Use disposable items whenever possible.
- Follow hygienic practices.
- Maintain a high standard of personal hygiene.

Hygiene equipment

Equipment	Hygiene practise
Head-band	A clean, freshly laundered head-band should be provided for each client to prevent cross-infection. Several should be available to allow for drying time
Gowns and towels 	All towels should be boil washed to destroy harmful micro-organisms following use. Clean towels and gowns should be provided for each client to prevent cross-infection
Treatment couch or beauty chair 	The treatment couch should have an easy-to-clean surface. It should be cleaned daily with warm water and detergent. The surface of the treatment couch should be protected with clean towels and clean disposable paper roll for each client
Magnifying lamp 	Check that the glass lens is cleaned after use
Spatula 	Throw away after use
Workstation surface	Clean with a chemical disinfectant. Protect with clean disposable paper roll.

Ellisons

Ellisons

Sorisa

Sorisa

Ellisons

Preparation of the therapist

Ensure that the treatment area is warm and comfortable and that lighting is adequate to induce relaxation, and to ensure that the treatment is performed competently. Check that the area is free from obstacles that could cause a fall.

Sanitise the hands, to remove surface dirt, this will also show the client you have good hygiene practice.

Check the work area to make sure you have all the equipment, products and materials you require for the facial treatment. Use the checklist provided on page 90–1.

Preparing the client – the consultation

The consultation should be carried out in the privacy of a treatment cubicle. It should take place when the client first meets you. The consultation enables the therapist to:

- assess whether the client is suitable for treatment or whether treatment is contra-indicated in some way
- ask the client specific questions about the current skin-care routine and general health. The client's answers will suggest to the therapist what is required, and what is achievable, from a skin-care programme.

During the consultation the therapist can also explain what is involved in the treatment, how long it takes and what after-care and home-care is required.

Also during the consultation, the client will:

- discover what the beauty therapist can offer
- ask questions and receive honest professional advice concerning the most appropriate choice of skin-care product
- confirm and agree the treatment aim.

At the end of the consultation the client should fully understand what the proposed treatment involves:

1 Ask the client to remove jewellery from the treatment area, to prevent it becoming soiled by facial products. Place the jewellery in view of the client, usually in a tissue-lined bowl.

2 Offer the client a gown to wear. Position the client into a comfortable and relaxed position for treatment. The couch or beauty chair should offer adequate back support and be comfortable. Cover the client with a large bath towel. Drape a small hand towel across their shoulders.

3 Fasten a clean head-band around the client's hairline. Position the head-band so that it does not cover the skin of the face.

4 After preparing the client, wash your hands: this demonstrates to the client your concern to work hygienically.

5 Check with the senior therapist that your facial treatment plan meets their satisfaction.

TIP

Work area
The work area should be left ready for the next client on treatment completion.
Waste products should be disposed of correctly.
If you are free, assist other colleagues to tidy the area after treatment to maintain the work area in readiness for the next client.

Basic facial treatment procedure

Briefly, the stages in the basic facial treatment procedure are:

- skin cleansing
- toning
- application of a face mask
- moisturiser application.

Skin cleansing treatment

There are two parts in the cleansing routine:

1 The **superficial cleanse** uses lightweight cleansing preparations to emulsify surface make-up, dirt and grease.

2 The **deep cleanse** uses a heavier cleansing product – often a cream – which allows massage movements to be applied to the skin without the cleansing product evaporating.

Superficial cleansing
The face is cleansed in the following order:

1 the eye tissue and lashes
2 the lips
3 the neck, chin, cheeks and forehead.

STEP-BY-STEP

1 Wash your hands
2 Cleanse the eye area using a suitable eye make-up remover.
3 Each eye is cleansed separately supporting the delicate eye tissue with the non-working hand. Apply eye make-up remover (oily or non-oily) directly to clean, damp cotton wool. First, stroke down the length of the lashes, then cleanse the eye tissue in a sweeping circle, outwards across the upper eyelid, circling beneath the lower lashes towards the nose. Repeat, changing the cotton wool regularly until the eye area and cotton wool shows clean. Any make-up left along the lash line should be removed with a clean cotton bud.
4 Cleanse the lips, preferably with a cleansing milk or lotion. Apply a little product to damp cotton wool. Wipe the cleanser across the lips. Support the corner of the mouth with the non-working hand. Repeat, changing regularly the cotton wool until the lip area and cotton wool shows clean.
5 Select a cleansing product to suit your clients skin type:

Whichever cleanser is chosen, it should have the following qualities:

- it should cleanse the skin effectively without causing irritation
- it should remove all traces of make-up and grease

- it should feel pleasant to use
- it should be easy to remove from the skin.

Skin type	Cleansing product
Oily	Foaming cleanser / Cleansing lotion
Dry	Cleansing milk / Cleansing cream
Combination	Foaming cleanser / Cleansing lotion / Cleansing milk

6 Apply the cleanser to the client's skin using your hands – sufficient to cover the face and neck – and massage gently over the surface of the skin. Using a series of light, circular movements with the fingertips, gently massage the product into the skin, beginning at the base of the neck and finishing at the forehead.

7 Remove the cleanser thoroughly, in an upwards and outwards direction, with clean damp cotton wool or facial sponges dampened with clean, warm water if preferred.

8 Repeat this process until all excess cleanser has been removed.

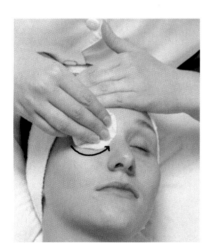

Cleansing the eye area

Cleansing the lips

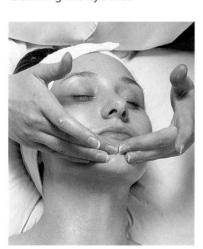

Cleansing the face

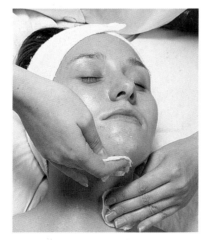

Removing cleanser

Deep cleansing

The deep cleanse involves a series of massage movement using the hands and cleansing product. The skin becomes warm during the massage, which aids the absorption of the cleanser into the hair follicles and pores and increases the cleansing action:

STEP-BY-STEP

1 Select and apply a suitable cleanser to the face and neck.

2 Stroke up both sides of the neck, using your fingertips. At the chin, draw the fingers outwards at the angle of the jaw and lightly stroke down to the neck to the starting position.

3 Apply small circular movements over the skin of the face and neck.

4 Draw the fingertips outwards to the angle of the jaw. Rest each index finger against the jaw bone. Place the middle finger beneath the jaw bone. Move the right hand towards the chin. When the index finger glides over the chin, return the fingers to the starting position beneath the jaw bone. Repeat with the left hand.

5 Apply circular movements, starting at the chin, working up towards the nose and finishing at the temples. Slide the fingers from the temples back to the chin, and repeat.

6 Position the ring finger of the right hand at the bridge of the nose. Perform a running movement, sliding the ring, middle and index fingers off the end of the nose. Repeat immediately with the left hand.

7 With the ring fingers, trace a circle around the eye. Begin at the inner corner of the upper brow bone; slide to the outer corners of the brow bone, around and under the eyes, and return to the starting position.

8 Using both hands, apply small circular movements across the forehead.

9 Open the index and middle fingers of each hand and perform a criss-cross stroking movement over the forehead.

10 Slide the index fingers upwards slightly, lifting the inner eyebrow. Lift the centre of the eyebrow with the middle finger. Finally, lift the outer corner of eyebrow with the ring finger. Slide the ring fingers around the outer corner and beneath the eye.

11 With the pads of each hand, apply slight pressure at the temples. This indicates to the client that the cleansing sequence is complete.

12 Remove the cleansing product from the skin, using damp cotton wool or facial sponges.

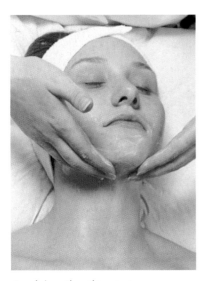

Applying the cleanser

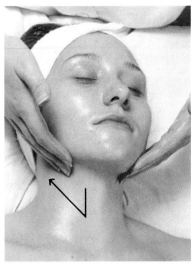

Stroking up the sides of the neck

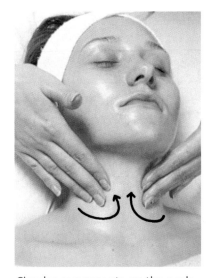

Circular movements on the neck

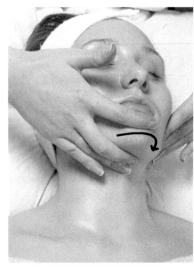

Stroking the jaw bone and chin

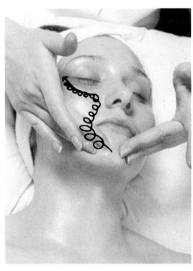

Circular movements to the chin, nose and temples

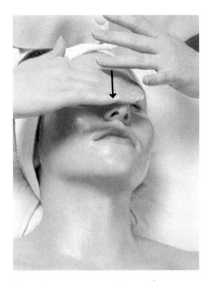

Running movements on the nose

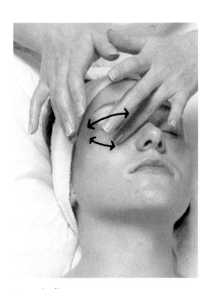

Eye circling

Circular movements on the forehead

Criss-cross stroking of the forehead

Lifting the eyebrows

> **TIP** ✔
>
> **Combination skin**
> If preferred, different toning lotions can be applied to treat the different skin types of a combination skin.

Skin toning

After the skin has been cleansed it is the toned with an appropriate lotion. Whichever toning lotion is chosen it should have the following qualities:

- it should produce a cooling effect on the skin when the water or alcohol evaporates from the skin's surface
- it should create a skin-tightening effect on the skin. This reduces the flow of sebum and sweat onto the skin's surface.

Skin type	Toning lotion
Oily	**Astringents**, the strongest toning lotions with a high alcohol content to stimulate and promote skin healing
Dry	Skin bracer **Skin fresheners** the mildest toning lotions, containing little or no alcohol They consist of mainly purified water and floral extracts for their toning properties
Combination	**Skin tonic**, slightly stronger toning lotion that bracers and fresheners. Might contain a little of an astringent agent

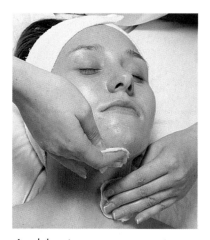

Applying toner

Toner application

1 Apply the selected toner to two pieces of clean damp cotton wool, which are wiped gently upwards and outwards over the surface of the skin.

2 The toner can be applied under pressure as a fine spray, using a vaporiser. This produces a fine mist of the toning lotion over the skin. Protect the eye tissue with damp cotton wool if using this technique.

3 After toner application, blot the skin dry with a soft facial tissue. Make a small tear in the centre of the tissue, for the client's nose. Place the tissue over the face and neck and mould it to the skin to absorb excess moisture.

The skin can be inspected at this stage using a cold light magnifier to illuminate the skins surface to identify further facial characteristics.

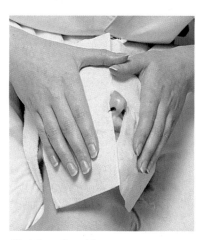

Blotting the skin

Mask treatment

The face mask is applied when the skin has been thoroughly cleansed and toned. It is usually applied as the final facial treatment because of its cleansing, refining and soothing effects upon the skin. Select the appropriate mask ingredients to treat the skin type. There are two types of mask:

- **setting** masks: are applied in a thin layer over the skins surface and are then allowed to dry
- **non-setting** masks: stay soft on application; they do not tighten like a setting mask.

You are required to competently apply a non-setting mask.

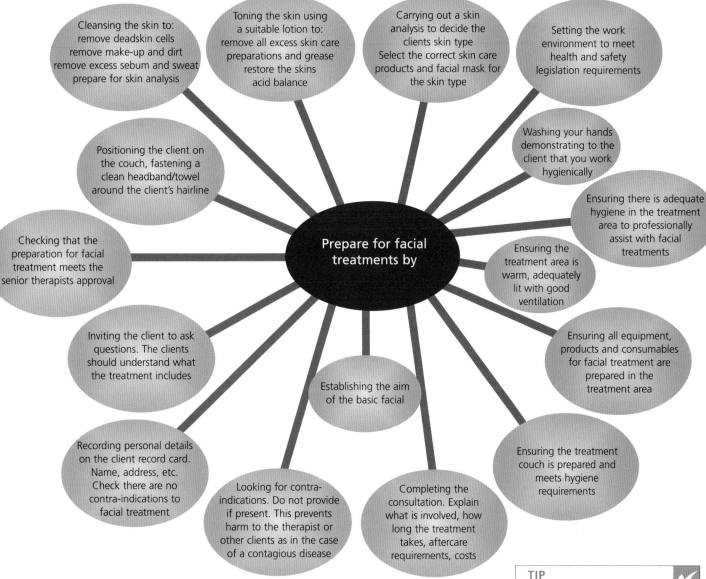

Cleansing the skin to:
remove deadskin cells
remove make-up and dirt
remove excess sebum and sweat
prepare for skin analysis

Toning the skin using
a suitable lotion to:
remove all excess skin care
preparations and grease
restore the skins
acid balance

Carrying out a skin
analysis to decide the
clients skin type
Select the correct skin care
products and facial mask for
the skin type

Setting the work
environment to meet
health and safety
legislation requirements

Positioning the client on
the couch, fastening a
clean headband/towel
around the client's hairline

Washing your hands
demonstrating to the
client that you work
hygienically

Checking that the
preparation for facial
treatment meets the
senior therapists approval

**Prepare for facial
treatments by**

Ensuring there is adequate
hygiene in the treatment
area to professionally
assist with facial
treatments

Ensuring the
treatment area is
warm, adequately
lit with good
ventilation

Inviting the client to ask
questions. The clients
should understand what
the treatment includes

Establishing the aim
of the basic facial

Ensuring all equipment,
products and consumables
for facial treatment are
prepared in the
treatment area

Recording personal details
on the client record card.
Name, address, etc.
Check there are no
contra-indications to
facial treatment

Looking for contra-
indications. Do not provide
if present. This prevents
harm to the therapist or
other clients as in the case
of a contagious disease

Completing the
consultation. Explain
what is involved, how
long the treatment
takes, aftercare
requirements, costs

Ensuring the treatment
couch is prepared and
meets hygiene
requirements

> **TIP** ✔
>
> **Pre-prepared treatment mask**
> This type of mask is often available for retail sale to the client and will enable the client to continue to care for the skin at home

Non-setting mask

These are preprepared and have a softening and moisturising effect on the skin. Each mask contains various biological extracts or chemical substances to treat different skin conditions. Instructions will be provided with the mask, stating how the product is to be used professionally.

Mask application

The method of mask preparation, application and removal are different for the various mask types. The guidelines below are for a non-setting, preprepared mask.

1 Select the non-setting mask suited to the client's skin type. Always read the manufacturer's instructions before applying.

> **TIP** ✔
>
> **Maintaining the working area**
> It is important to work in a hygienic, organised manner, leaving the workstation neat and tidy and removing all waste materials both during and at the end of the treatment.

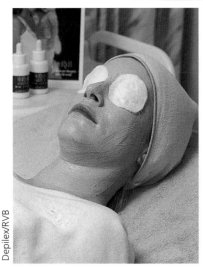

A face mask treatment

2 Discuss the treatment procedure with the client, in particular:

- what the mask will feel like on application
- what sensation the client is likely to experience
- how long the mask will be left on the skin.

Generally, the mask will be left in place for 10–20 minutes.

3 Using the sanitised mask brush, begin to apply the mask. The usual sequence of the mask application is neck, chin, cheeks, nose and forehead. Apply the mask evenly and quickly so that it has maximum effect on the whole face. Don't apply it too thickly; as well as making mask removal difficult it is wasteful as only the part that is in contact with skin has any effect. Keep the mask clear of the nostrils, the lips, the eyebrows and the hairline.

4 Apply dampened cotton wool pads over the eyes to relax the client.

5 Leave the mask for the recommended treatment time and according to the effect required.

6 Wash your hands.

7 When the mask is ready for removal, remove the eye pads.

8 Remove the mask using mask removal sponges, which should be damp – not wet – for client comfort and so that water does not run into the client eyes nose and hairline.

9 When the mask is thoroughly removed, apply the appropriate toning lotion. Blot the skin dry with a facial tissue.

Moisturiser application follows.

Skin moisturising

The basic formulation of a moisturiser is oil and water to make an oil-in-water emulsion. The water content helps to return lost moisture to the surface layers of the skin; the oil content prevents moisture loss from the surface of the skin. Often, a **humectant** ingredient is included, such as **glycerine**, which attracts moisture from the surrounding air and stops the moisturiser from drying out.

Moisturisers are available for wear during the day or night and are available in different formulations to suit different skin types. Select a moisturising day product to suit your client's skin type.

Skin type	Moisturiser
Oily	Moisturising lotion
Dry	Moisturising cream
Combination	Moisturising lotion

Whichever moisturiser is chosen, it should have the following qualities:

- it should soften the skin and relieve skin tightness and sensitivity
- it should plump out the skin's tissues with moisture, minimising the appearance of fine lines.

Moisturiser application

Moisturiser is applied after the final application of toning lotion.

1 Place a small amount of moisturiser in the palms of the hands. If the product is in a jar, remove the moisturiser with a clean spatula.

2 Apply moisturiser on small dots to the neck, chin, cheeks, nose and forehead. Spread it quickly and evenly in a fine film over the face, using light upwards and outward stroking movements.

3 Blot excess moisturiser from the skin using a facial tissue.

Applying moisturiser

Spreading moisturiser evenly to the face and neck

Treatment time 45 minutes

Giving due care and consideration to health and safety legislation throughout treatment

Using facial skin care products as per manufacturers guidelines and treatment requirements

Carry out facial treatments by

Applying a face mask to achieve a desirable effect on the skin;
- cleansing
- toning
- nourishing
- refreshing

Applying moisturiser to:
- keep the skin lubricated and prevent water loss
- reduce sensitivity
- protect it from external environmental damage i.e. UV
- provides a barrier between the skin and further facial cosmetics

Toning the skin using a suitable lotion to:
- remove all excess skincare preparations/grease
- restore the skins acid balance

Removal of mask using sterile sponges following recommended application time

Completing facial treatments

Make sure the client's records are up to date at the end of the treatment. This is important when you need to refer to them in the future. The record should then be stored securely.

The client should be given homecare advice so that the skin can be cared for at home. This will be different for each client, depending on individual needs.

Basic home-care and advice

- Warn the client that a few blemishes might be experienced. These are caused by the cleansing action of the facial.
- If a client is given a sample of a treatment product, explain its correct use in terms of application and removal so that the client can gain maximum benefit from the product.
- Recommend the skin is cleansed and toned, twice a day, morning and night. Advice on the correct products to use.
- A moisturiser should be applied for day use and a separate moisturiser applied for night use. Each is formulated to achieve a different treatment effect. Advise on the correct products to use.
- The skin should be toned and moisturised following mask application.

Advise the client that the correct treatment interval between facial treatments is usually 14–28 days.

Promoting products

Providing advice also gives you the opportunity to recommend retail products. This enhances the salon's retail sales and profit.

Contra-action

Ask clients to contact the salon immediately and speak with the senior therapist if any unwanted reaction to the treatment occurs. Such *contra-actions* (e.g. an allergy, recognised by redness, swelling and inflammation) should be noted on the client's record for future reference.

TIP

Moisturiser formulations
Moisturising lotions contain 85–90% water and 10–15% oil
Moisturising creams contain 70–85% water and 10–15% oil
Hypo-allergenic moisturisers are available for clients with sensitive skins. These are screened for all known common sensitising agents, such as lanolin and perfume.

TIP

Moisturiser ingredients
Many moisturisers contain ingredients that improve the condition of the skin, such as vitamin E – an excellent skin conditioner – or ultraviolet filters to protect the skin from the premature ageing effects of sunlight.

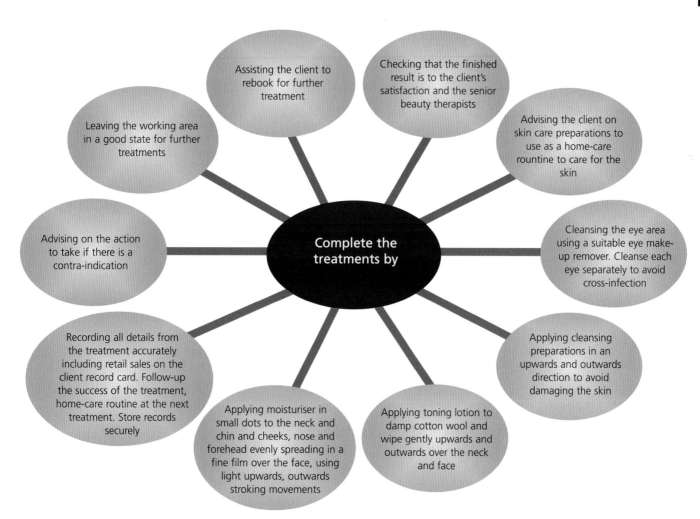

Complete the treatments by:

- Assisting the client to rebook for further treatment
- Checking that the finished result is to the client's satisfaction and the senior beauty therapists
- Advising the client on skin care preparations to use as a home-care rountine to care for the skin
- Leaving the working area in a good state for further treatments
- Cleansing the eye area using a suitable eye make-up remover. Cleanse each eye separately to avoid cross-infection
- Advising on the action to take if there is a contra-indication
- Applying cleansing preparations in an upwards and outwards direction to avoid damaging the skin
- Recording all details from the treatment accurately including retail sales on the client record card. Follow-up the success of the treatment, home-care routine at the next treatment. Store records securely
- Applying moisturiser in small dots to the neck and chin and cheeks, nose and forehead evenly spreading in a fine film over the face, using light upwards, outwards stroking movements
- Applying toning lotion to damp cotton wool and wipe gently upwards and outwards over the neck and face

Glossary

Acid mantle	acid film on the skin's surface created by a combination of sweat and sebum. The acid mantle is protective and discourages the growth of bacteria and fungi
Aftercare advice	recommended advice given to the client following treatment to continue the benefits of the treatment
Allergen	a substance that the skin is sensitive to and which causes an allergic reaction
Blood	nutritive liquid circulating through the blood vessels; transports essential nutrients to the cells and removes waste products; transports other important substances such as oxygen and hormones
Cell	the smallest and simplest unit capable of life
Cleanser	a skin-care preparation that removes dead skin cells, excess sweat and sebum, make-up and dirt from the skin's surface to maintain a healthy skin complexion

Glossary

Consultation	assessment of a client's needs using different assessment techniques, including questioning and natural observation
Contra-action	an unwanted reaction occurring during or after treatment application
Contra-indication	a problematic symptom that means that treatment might not proceed
Cross-infection	the transfer of contagious micro-organisms
Data Protection Act (1998)	legislation designed to protect client privacy and confidentiality
Deep cleanse	uses a heavier-than-usual cleansing product – often a cream – that allows massage movements to be applied to the skin without the cleansing product evaporating
Dermis	the inner portion of the skin, situated underneath the epidermis
Epidermis	the outer layer of the skin
Facial	a treatment to improve the appearance, condition and functioning of the skin and underlying structures
Fibres	found in the dermis and give the skin its strength and elasticity. Yellow elastin gives the skin its elasticity, white collagen gives skin its strength
Fungus	microscopic plants that in humans, are parasites. Fungal diseases of the skin feed of the waste products of the skin. They are found on the skin's surface or they can attack deeper tissues.
Hair follicle	an appendage (structure) in the skin formed from epidermal tissue. Cells move up the hair follicle from the bottom (the hair bulb), changing in structure, to form the hair
Hygiene	the recommended standard of cleanliness necessary in the salon to prevent cross-infection and secondary infection
Lymph	a clear, straw-coloured liquid circulating in the lymph vessels and lymphatics of the body, filtered out of the blood plasma.
Mask	a skin-cleansing treatment preparation applied to the skin. It might contain different ingredients to have a deep cleansing, toning, nourishing or refreshing effect. It can be applied to the hands, feet and face

Glossary

Massage	manipulation of the soft tissues of the body, producing heat and stimulating the muscular, circulatory and nervous system
Melanin	a pigment in the skin that contributes to skin colour
Melanocytes	cells that produce the skin pigment melanin, which contributes to skin colour
Moisturiser	a skin-care preparation (formulation of oil and water) that helps maintain the skin's natural moisture by locking moisture into the skin, offering protection and hydration
Muscle	contractile tissue responsible for movement of the body
Muscle tone	the normal degree of tension in healthy muscle
Nerve	a collection of single neurons surrounded by a protective sheath through which impulses are transmitted between the brain or spinal cord and another part of the body
Papillae	projections near the surface of the dermis, which contain nerve endings and blood capillaries. These supply the upper epidermis with nutrition
Record cards	confidential cards recording personal details of each client registered at the salon
Sanitisation	the destruction of some, but not all, living micro-organisms
Sebaceous gland	a minute sac-like organ usually associated with the hair follicle. The cells of the gland decompose and produce the sebum. Found all over the body except the soles of the feet and the palms of the hands
Sebum	the skin's natural oil, which keeps the skin supple
Secondary infection	bacterial penetration into the skin causing infection
Skin allergy	if the skin is sensitive to a particular substance an allergic skin reaction will occur. This is recognised by irritation, swelling and inflammation
Skin analysis	assessment of the clients skin type and condition
Skin appendages	structures within the skin including sweat glands (that excrete sweat), hair follicles (that produce hair), sebaceous glands (that produce sebum) and nails – a horny substance that protects the ends of the fingers.
Skin tone	the strength and elasticity of the skin

Glossary

Skin type	the different physiological functioning of each persons skin provides their skin type. Skin types include dry (lacking in oil), oily (excessive oil) and combination (a mixture of the other two skin types)
Sterilisation	the total destruction of all micro-organisms
Subcutaneous tissue	a layer of fatty tissue situated below the epidermis and dermis
Superficial cleanse	uses light-weight cleansing preparations to emulsify surface make-up, dirt and grease
Sweat glands	small structures in the skin of the dermis and epidermis that excrete sweat. Their function is to regulate body temperature through the evaporation of sweat from the skin surface
Toning lotion	a skin-care preparation to remove all traces of cleanser from the skin. It produces a cooling effect on the skin and has a skin tightening effect
Treatment plan	after the consultation, suitable treatment objectives are established to treat the client's condition and needs
Virus	virus particles invade healthy body cells and multiply within the cell. Eventually the virus kills the cell – the cell walls break down and the virus particles are freed to attack further cells

Assessment and knowledge of understanding

Unit BT2: Assist with facial treatments

You have now learned about the different products and treatments that you can apply to the skin of the face and neck, this will enable you to assist with facial treatments. To test your level of knowledge and understanding, answer the following short questions, these will prepare you for your summative (final) assessment.

Anatomy and physiology:

1 Name three functions of the skin.

2 How many layers of the epidermis are there?

3 What is the dermis?

4 Where is the dermis situated?

5 Label the features of the cross-section of the skin shown below:

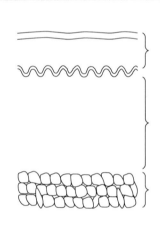

Prepare for facial treatments:

1 What details should be recorded on the client's record card?

2 At the consultation you notice a client has a watery eye, what action do you take?

3 How do you identify a client's skin type and treatment requirements?

4 How should all client records be stored to comply with the Data Protection Act (1998)?

5 Name four facial conditions that would contra-indicate treatment.

6 How should you prepare yourself for the treatment (remember to considering health and safety requirements)?

7 How can you ensure client comfort when preparing the facial treatment area?

Assessment and knowledge of understanding

Carry out facial treatments:

1 How long would you allow for a complete basic facial treatment?

2 Design a facial treatment, lasting one hour, for a client with a dry skin type. Describe:

    a the aim of the facial treatment
    b the facial skin products you are going to use
    c the aftercare advice to be given to maintain the skin condition.

Consider what products the client should be recommended to use at home and how to use them.

3 Why is it important to keep accurate records of the client's treatment?

4 What is the purpose of the following skin-care products?

    a cleanser
    b toning lotion
    c moisturiser
    d face mask.

Complete the treatments:

1 What skin-care products would you recommend that a client use as part of her homecare routine?

2 How would you explain to the client the correct application and – where relevant – removal of the following products for home use?

    a cleansing milk
    b toning lotion
    c non-setting face mask.

3 How often would you recommend a basic facial treatment?

4 How should the treatment are be left following each treatment, and why?

chapter 5

ASSIST WITH NAIL TREATMENTS ON THE HANDS

BT3

Learning objectives

This chapter covers the skills and knowledge you need to assist with and provide basic nail treatments on the hands. It describes the competencies to enable you to:

- prepare for nail treatments

- carry out nail treatments

- complete the treatments.

When performing nail treatments, it is important at all times to consider health and safety using the knowledge you gained from Unit G1: Ensure your own actions reduce risks to health and safety (see Chapter 1).

The table shown will help you to check your progress in gaining the necessary practical skills and knowledge for Unit BT3: Assist with nail treatments on the hands. Tick (✓), when you feel you have gained your practical skills and knowledge in the following areas:

		✓
1	The treatment aim of a basic nail treatment	
2	Contra-indications which prevent a nail treatment	
3	Equipment and products needed	
4	Preparing the treatment area	
5	Preparing yourself before the nail treatment	
6	Client consultation and preparing the client	
7	How to carry out the basic nail treatment	
8	After-care and advice for the client	
9	Contra-actions to the nail treatment	

When you have ticked all the areas you can ask your assessor to assess you on Unit 3: Assist with nail treatments on the hands. After practical assessment, your assessor might decide that you still need to practice further to improve your skills. If so, your assessor will tell you how and where you need to improve to gain competence.

INTRODUCTION

The basic nail treatment aims to improve the appearance of the:

- hands
- cuticles
- nails.

The hands

Healthy hands have soft, smooth skin. Wear and tear, or neglect, can make the skin dry, chapped, irritated, rough and even broken.

When carrying out basic nail treatment, your aim is to maintain or return the skin to a healthy, soft and smooth condition. This might take more than one treatment and you will need to advice the client on how to care for the hands at home; this is called after-care and advice.

The cuticles

The cuticle is the part of the skin found around the base of the nail. When in a good condition, the cuticle is soft and loose. However, it easily becomes dry, tight, split and overgrown at the base of the nail.

When carrying out the basic nail treatment, your aim is to soften and moisturise the cuticles. After-care advice must always be given so that clients know how to care for the cuticles themselves.

ACTIVITY

Skin conditions on the hand
Why can the skin on the hands become dry, chapped, irritated, rough or broken?
You need to ask the client questions to find out a cause for the skin conditions appearance, and then you can give helpful advice.
Discuss with your salon colleagues possible causes.

The nails

The nails should be smooth, supple and have a healthy pink appearance. The edge that is filed (the free edge) should be even in shape. The nails can lose their healthy pink colour and become ridged, pitted, brittle and bruised, and the free edge is easily split and broken.

When carrying out the basic nail treatment, your aim is to maintain or improve the healthy pink colour of the nail, improve the smoothness and suppleness of the nail and file the free edge to a suitable even, shape and length.

After-care advice must always be given so that clients know how to care for the nails themselves.

You need to know about the different parts of the nail if you are to be able to improve its appearance and care properly for the nail.

ANATOMY AND PHYSIOLOGY

All about the nail its structure and function

The basic nail unit

Nails grow from the ends of the fingers and toes and their main purpose is to form a hard protective shield.

Matrix

The matrix is found at the bottom of the nails and is the growing area of the nail. It is made up of **cells** – tiny particles that make up all living things. The cells divide to produce the nail plate.

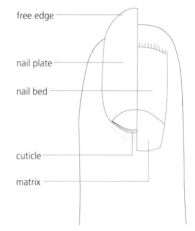

The structure of the nail

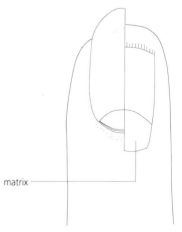

The matrix

The nail plate

The nail plate is the correct name for the part of the nail that covers the **nail bed**, the portion of skin on which the nail plate rests. The cells here are clear and have become hardened. These hard cells serve to protect the nail bed below and, because they are clear, allow you to see if the living nail bed is a healthy pink colour. The function of the nail plate is to protect the nail bed.

The nail grows forward slowly over the nail bed, at a rate of 0.5 mm to 1.2 mm per week. It takes between 4 and 6 months for a nail plate to grow fully from cuticle to free edge.

The nail bed

The nail bed is the part of the skin covered by the nail plate. The nail plate and nail bed separate at the free-edge end of the finger. The nail bed is made up of living cells and contains many **blood vessels**, which provide the nourishment necessary for healthy growth and repair; the nail bed also contains **nerves** that send messages to the central nervous system. The functions of the nail bed are to supply nourishment and protection (by means of nerve impulses).

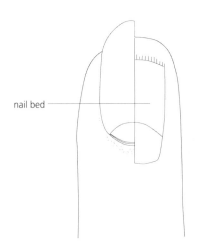

The nail bed

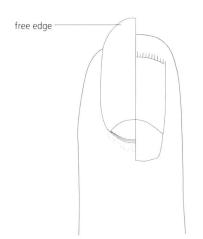

The free edge

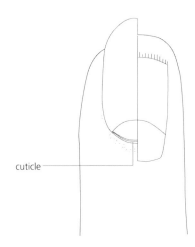

The cuticle

Cuticle

The cuticle is the overlapping skin at the bottom of the nail plate that grows forward onto the nail plate. When overgrown, it can grow high up onto the nail plate and will often split, which can then become infected. It is important to keep the cuticles soft and loose. The function of the cuticle is to protect the nail plate from infection

Free edge

The free edge is the part of the nail that grows beyond the fingertip. It is usually white, as it does not have the pink nail bed below it. It is the part of the nail that is filed and shaped. The function of the free edge is to protect the fingertip.

Nail shapes

Each clients hand size, finger length and nail shape is unique to them. It is important that the nail shape and length selected suits the client's hands and fingers. The nail plate free edge can be shaped to improve the appearance of the hands and fingers. Nail shapes include:

- Oval: the sides of the free edge are curved. This is an ideal shape for short, stubby fingers as it makes the fingers appear slimmer and longer.
- Square: the free edge is filed straight across. This nail shape will improve the appearance of thin, long fingers, making the fingers appear shorter and fuller.
- Squoval: a combination of oval and square nail shape. The nail is filed to a square finish at the free edge and is then gently curved at the corners.
- Round nails: the free edge is rounded and is an ideal shape for short nails, this style is popular with male clients.
- Pointed: avoid pointed nails shapes as this shape weakens the strength of the nail at the sides and it breaks easily.
- Fan: the nail becomes broader as it grows towards the free edge, appearing as a fan shape. The wider sides of the nail at the free edge should be shaped to achieve an oval shape.

<table>
<tr><td>TIP ✔</td></tr>
<tr><td>Pain
There are no blood vessels or nerves in the nail plate and free edge: this is why it can be cut without pain or bleeding.</td></tr>
</table>

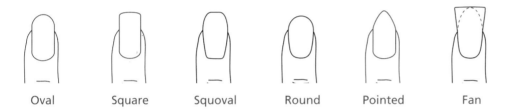

Oval   Square   Squoval   Round   Pointed   Fan

NAIL TREATMENT

A basic nail treatment includes:

When a client makes an appointment for a basic nail treatment, the receptionist should ask a few basic questions:

- What is the client's name and telephone number? This will help you to get the client record card ready before they arrive for treatment. The telephone number is important in case you need to cancel the treatment for any reason, i.e. the beauty therapist is ill.
- Which therapist does the client want to see? If a particular therapist is needed you will have to check on availability.
- When does the client want the treatment, i.e. day/date and time? If any of these are not available, suggest another time or day as near to this as possible.
- Has the client had the treatment before? This allows the client to ask you questions about the treatment.

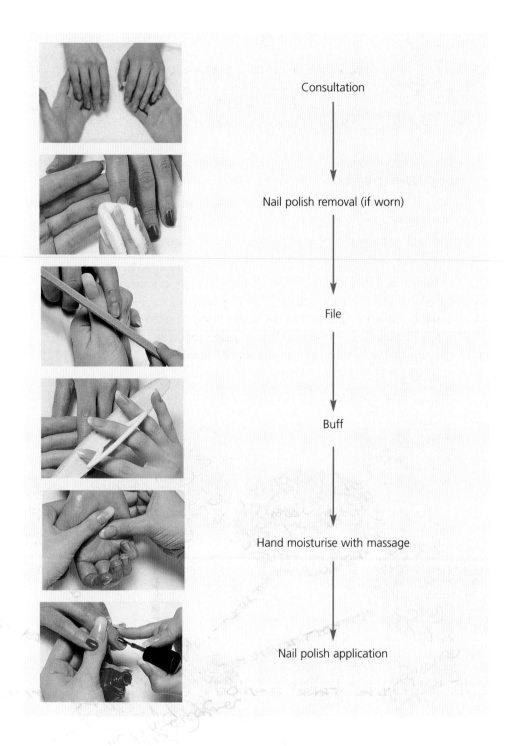

Consultation

Nail polish removal (if worn)

File

Buff

Hand moisturise with massage

Nail polish application

- Does the client require any other services in addition to the basic nail treatment? Always look at opportunities to increase treatment bookings, the salon needs to keep busy!

Remember, when making an appointment it is important to allow enough time to complete the treatment properly. It is also important for the therapist to be able to complete the treatment in the time allowed.

Allow 30 minutes for a basic nail treatment.

ACTIVITY

Treatment times
What is the time allowed for a basic nail treatment?
Why is it important to complete the treatment in this time?
Think of three reasons for both.

The Data Protection Act (1998)

A client's personal details are confidential, or private. All information relating to a client should be stored securely. Only those staff with permission to access it can do so. Therefore, as soon as all treatment details have been recorded on the record card, the client's details should be stored securely.

Before treatment

Contra-indications to treatment

Certain nail, hand and skin conditions prevent you from performing the basic nail treatment, these are known as **contra-indications**. If, when looking at a client's hands and nails before the treatment you think you recognise any of the following conditions, you must not perform basic nail treatment. You will need to refer the client tactfully to the relevant person in the salon for confirmation that the treatment can go ahead (or not).

HEALTH AND SAFETY

Contra-indications
Remember, you might be wrong when you think you have a client with a contra-indication. Always check – the client may be able to have the treatment after all.
Never diagnose, and try to avoid causing the client embarrassment.

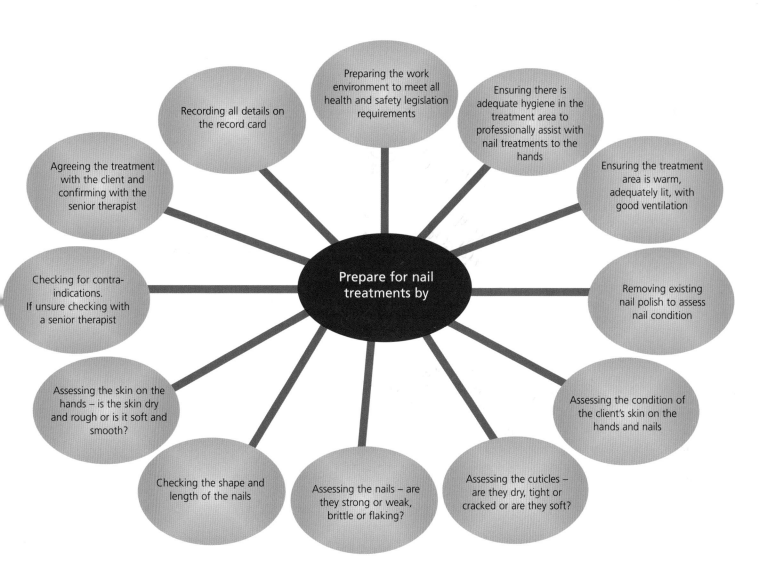

Contra-indications that prevent treatment

All the skin and nail conditions listed below are contagious – they can be passed to other clients and clients with these conditions should never be treated.

Name of contra-indication	Cause	Appearance
Impetigo 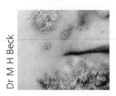	A **contagious** bacterial infection caused by minute, single-celled organisms and which results in **skin** inflammation	The skin appears red and is itchy. Small blisters appear, which burst and then form crusts
Warts: **Common wart**: found on the hand **Plane wart**: found on the fingers or either surface of the hands 	Contagious **viral** infection that results in abnormal skin growth A contagious **fungal** infection of the skin. Fungal diseases of the skin feed of the waste products of the skin	Skin growth, varying in size, shape, texture and colour. Usually raised with a rough surface. Found on the fingers, either surface of the hand
Scabies or **itch mites** 	A contagious **infestation** caused by an **animal parasite** that burrows beneath the skin and enters the hair follicles	Small lumps and wavy greyish lines appear on the skin. This is where dirt has entered where the parasite burrows under the skin. Found in warm, loose areas of skin such as in between the fingers, and the creases of the elbows
Tinea Corporis or **body ringworm** 	A contagious **fungal** infection of the skin, caused by microscopic plants. Fungal diseases of the skin feed off the waste products of the skin and are parasitic	Small, scaly red patches spread outwards and then heal from the centre, leaving a ring. Found on the limbs
Tinea unguium or **nail ringworm**	A contagious **fungal** infection of the nail plate	The nail plate is yellowish-grey. Eventually the nail plate becomes brittle and separates from the nail bed

Dr M H Beck

HEALTH AND SAFETY ✚

Broken skin

If a client has a minor, small scratch of the skin in the treatment area, treatment can usually go ahead by avoiding contact with the area, with permission of the senior therapist. If the client has a cut, redness and swelling the treatment should not go ahead. If unsure, seek guidance from the senior therapist first.

Nail and skin conditions that might restrict treatment

The nail skin conditions below are non-contagious and cannot be passed to other clients. You can therefore treat a client with one of these conditions, although you might need to adapt your treatment application.

Name of contra-indication	Cause	Appearance	Treatment
Bruised nail	Damage to the nail (e.g. by trapping in a door)	Part or all of the nail plate appears blue or black	Avoid the nail that is bruised when carrying out the nail treatment
Onychopagy	Excessive nail biting	Very little nail plate. The skin appears red and swollen due to biting of the skin around the nails	Regular weekly nail treatments to encourage nail growth and treat any dry skin and cuticle. The client could try applying bitter-tasting nail preparations at home to prevent nail biting
Pterygium	Neglect	Overgrown cuticles, tightly attached to the nail plate. When left untreated they often split and crack	Advice the client to have a manicure where the excess cuticle can be removed using specialised tools called *nippers* or ***clippers***. The client should be advised to apply a rich cuticle treatment cream daily
Ridges in the nail plate	Illness, damage or old age	Ridges in the nail plate running across or down the length of the nail plate, from the cuticle to the free edge. This can affect one or all nails	Buffing treatment to help to improve the appearance of the nail by smoothing out the ridges. A ridge-filling base coat can also be applied before nail polish application
Hangnail	Dry skin or cuticle that cracks. Biting the skin around the nail	The skin around the nail plate cracks and a small piece of skin appears between the nail plate and side of the nail (nail wall). Sometimes the area becomes red and swollen	Specialised manicure treatment to soften the skin and cuticles. Removal of the excess skin using cuticle nippers. Advise the client to apply hand cream and cuticle cream to prevent dryness
Leuconychia	Damage to the nail plate due to pressure or hitting with a hard object	White spots appear on the nail plate, which grow out with the nail	Advise the client to take general care of the nails. Recommend the application of a coloured nail polish to disguise the white spots

Dr A L Wright
Dr A L Wright
Dr A L Wright
Dr A L Wright
Judith Iford
Dr A L Wright

Name of contra-indication	Cause	Appearance	Treatment
Onychorrhexis	Poor diet Harsh detergents Incorrect choice/use of manicure products	Split, flaking nails	Ensure a balanced diet. Regular use of a hand cream. Protect the nails from detergents, which dry the nails, always wear rubber gloves. Nail treatment base polishes can have specific effects to improve the nail. Incorrect use/choice can dry the nails causing the nails to split and flake
Skin eczema	Inflammation of the skin caused by contact with a skin irritant	The skin becomes red, swells and blisters can appear. The blisters burst, which then causes scabs to form on the skin. Affects the inner creases of the elbows	Ensure you find out what irritants make the eczema worse and avoid contact with such products, e.g. perfumed products. The skin can benefit from massage lotion that contains soothing ingredients such as lavender. Do not treat if the skin is broken
Skin psoriasis	Cause unknown but becomes worse when the person is stressed Often hereditary	Itchy, red, flaky patches of skin, which can become infected if the skin becomes broken. Found on the elbows	The skin can benefit from massage lotion that contains soothing ingredients such as lavender. Do not treat if the skin is broken
Nail psoriasis	Psoriasis of the nail can cause further nail disorders to occur. Cause unknown but becomes worse when the person is stressed.Often hereditary	Pitting and discolouration of the nail plate with possible increased curvature, nail thickening and even loss	Take care when treating the nails It is advisable to keep the nails short
Broken bones	Injury – should be treated medically	The breakage might not be obvious. If the client is new, check that there have been no broken bones at the consultation	The broken bone must not be handled. Therefore, if one finger is broken you must avoid this finger. Always check first with the relevant person in the workplace

Dr A L Wright

Dr M H Beck

Dr M H Beck

HEALTH AND SAFETY

Skin disorders

If a client has a nail or skin disorder that has only recently appeared, ask that client to consult a GP on the suitability of nail treatment. This would be relevant for all contra-indications plus those conditions that restrict treatment, mainly eczema and psoriasis. Before treating any client, if you are at all unsure check with the relevant person in the workplace.

Pretreatment

Refer to the equipment and materials checklist to make sure that you have all that is required to perform a basic nail treatment.

EQUIPMENT AND MATERIALS CHECKLIST

Manicure table or trolley – on which to place everything ☐

Small bowls lined with tissues (2) – 1 for the client's jewellery and 1 for clean cotton wool ☐

Towels (2) – freshly laundered for each client ☐

Finger bowl to place the fingers in warm water to soften the cuticles ☐

Emery board to shape the free edge ☐

Orange sticks to remove products hygienically and to gently loosen the cuticle and clean under the free edge ☐

Nail polish remover to remove previous polish worn by the client. Also to remove any polish that is accidentally placed on the surrounding cuticle or skin. ☐

Coloured nail polish – a range of colours suited to the client's nails and choice ☐

Base coat ☐

Specialist nail treatment polishes, i.e. nail strengthener ☐

Top coat ☐

Nail scissors to reduce the length of the nail before filing ☐

Buffers to remove surface cells on the nail plate achieving a smoother nail plate and increasing blood circulation ☐

Buffing paste – a gritty paste used to remove surface cells and give a shine to the nail plate ☐

Client's record card to record all clients personal details and record details of the treatment ☐

Cotton wool to remove old nail enamel and excess oils from the nails before nail polish application ☐

Tissues to place over the sanitised nail equipment and line the bowls as necessary ☐

Waste bin or lined bowl for waste materials ☐

Sanitising solution to keep the small tools hygienic once sterilised ☐

Skin cleanser to cleanse the client's skin before you begin the treatment ☐

BEAUTY WORKS

Date	Therapist name

Client name	Date of birth

Address	Postcode

Evening phone number   Day phone number

Name of doctor   Doctor's address and phone number

Related medical history (conditions that may restrict or prohibit treatment application)

Are you taking any medication

CONTRA-INDICATIONS REQUIRING MEDICAL REFERRAL
(Preventing manicure treatment application)

☐ bacterial infection (i.e. paronychia)
☐ viral infection (i.e. plane warts)
☐ fungal infection (i.e. tinea ungium)
☐ severe nail separation
☐ severe eczema and psoriasis
☐ severe bruising

EQUIPMENT AND MATERIALS

☐ nail and skin treatment tools
☐ abrasives (e.g. buffing cream)
☐ nail and skin products
☐ nail conditioners (e.g. cuticle cream)
☐ skin conditioners (e.g. hand cream)
☐ consumables

NAIL FINISH

☐ buffing
☐ clear polish
☐ nail strengthener

CONTRA-INDICATIONS WHICH RESTRICT TREATMENT
(Treatment may require adaption)

☐ minor nail separation
☐ mild psoriasis/eczema
☐ recent scar tissue
☐ severely bitten
☐ severely damaged nails
☐ broken bones
☐ minor cuts and abrasions
☐ minor bruising and swelling

TREATMENT AIM

☐ improvement of skin condition

  products used

☐ improvement of nail condition

  products used

NAIL, CUTICLE AND SKIN CONDITION

nails	cuticle	skin
☐ normal	☐ dry	☐ dry
☐ brittle	☐ split	☐ hard
☐ dry	☐ overgrown	
☐ weak		

MASSAGE MEDIUMS

☐ creams
☐ oils

Beauty therapist signature (for reference)

Client signature (confirmation of details)

Equipment and products used in a basic nail treatment

Product	Use	Health and safety
Sanitising solution 	Sanitising liquid that prevents the multiplication of micro-organisms but does not kill all micro-organisms. Objects must be kept sanitary once sterilised	Could cause a slippage if spilt. Might cause skin irritation and be toxic if swallowed. Chemical sterilising sprays are also use to sterilise the surface of manicure tools. These should be used following manufacturer's instructions and in a well-ventilated area, avoiding contact with flame and excessive heat
Finger bowl 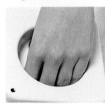	Fill with warm water and add a pleasant smelling nail soak to cleanse and soften the cuticles	Clean after use with a detergent, disinfectant, rinse and dry. When in use keep on a stable surface to avoid spillage
Emery board 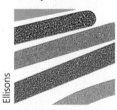	A nail file used to shape the nails. It usually has two sides, one side is coarser than the other	Use a new emery board for each client to avoid cross-infection. Use the coarser side to reduce length of the nail. Never use a sawing action when filing as you can cause the free edge to split
Orange sticks 	Disposable wooden tools, usually with a hoof-shaped end for use around the cuticle and a pointed end for cleaning under the free edge. They can also be used to remove product from containers	Never reuse the orange sticks, throw away after the treatment to avoid cross-infection. Always tip with clean cotton wool if used to clean under the free edge. Used incorrectly on the nail they could pierce the skin.
Nail scissors 	Used to shorten long nails before filing.	Support the nails at the side of the nail plate with the other hand to avoid client discomfort and ensure that all pieces of nail can be collected and thrown away. Sterilise nail scissors between each client to avoid cross-infection
Buffers 	Use to improve the surface appearance of the nail, stimulate blood circulation to the nail bed and impart shine to the nail plate. The buffer might have a plastic handle and a replaceable pad covered with soft leather. This buffer can be used with or without buffing paste. Also available are four-sided nail buffers, similar to a thick emery board with a choice of surfaces from slightly coarse to very smooth, these are used without buffing paste	Ensure that the soft leather cover is replaced for each client to avoid cross-infection. This means you will need more than one cover. Do not over-use the coarse buffer or the nail will become thin and weakened

Ellisons

Product	Use	Health and safety
Skin cleanser	A chemical that removes a number of harmful micro-organisms from the client's skin that could cause infection. This cleansing process is called sanitisation and an antiseptic product is often used	Antiseptics can be used safely on the skin but some clients might have an intolerance to them, leading to an allergic reaction. Always check at consultation if the client has any known skin allergies
Nail polish remover	A product that will dissolve and remove nail polish and grease from the nail plate. The ingredient that causes this is called *acetone*.	Nail polish remover can be drying to the nail: choose one that contains oils. Store away from heat as it is highly flammable
Nail polish: coloured basecoat topcoat	Can be applied to improve the natural appearance of the nail, or add colour and protection	Always secure the lid tightly after use to avoid the product spoiling and accidental spillage. Ensure that the client is not allergic, some clients have allergies to the ingredient *formaldehyde* in nail enamel
Nail strengthener	A nail polish product that strengthens a nail plate that has a tendency to split in layers, usually a dry, brittle nail	Check if the client has known allergies, some clients have allergies to the ingredient *formaldehyde*, which might is sometimes found in nail strengthener
Buffing paste	A coarse cream containing ingredients such as pumice or talc to remove the surface cells of the nail plates, giving shine	Avoid over-use of the buffing paste to avoid thinning and weakening of the nail plate
Hand cream/oil	A mixture of waxes and oils with perfumes and preservatives to maintain its quality. Hand creams/oils soften the skin of the hands and cuticles and assist the application of massage movements	Some hand massage products contain lanolin – a skin moisturising agent, that can cause an allergic skin reaction. Always check if the client has any known allergies before treatment, and know your product ingredients

Salon Systems

LONGER LASTING
NAIL COLOUR
WITH SILICA

MATTE
BASECOAT

Salon Systems

BASE, TOP AND
STRENGTHENER
WITH OPTICAL BRIGHTENER
salonsystem

3 IN 1

Salon Systems

hand defence
AGE DEFYING
HAND CREAM
PROTECTS & NOURISHES
WITH ADSAINE, MALLOW,
LIME BLOSSOM & SUNSCREENS

Sterilisation and sanitisation

It is important that hygienic practice is considered before and throughout the client treatment. This will help prevent cross-infection – the transfer of harmful bacteria/micro-organisms from one person to another.

Hygiene checks

- Ensure that all tools and equipment are clean and sterile before use.
- Disinfect work surfaces regularly.
- Use disposable items whenever possible.
- Follow hygienic practices.
- Maintain a high standard of personal hygiene.

Hygiene equipment

The autoclave
A sterilizing unit similar to a pressure cooker – creates steam as the water inside it boils. A temperature of 121–134°C is reached, which is sufficient to sterilise the items inside the autoclave. This process is only suitable for equipment that can withstand the heating process – always check first.
When possible, use equipment that can be thrown away after use (disposable), i.e. emery boards and orange sticks.

Equipment	Hygiene practise
Scissors	Clean with a disinfectant and autoclave. Store in ultraviolet cabinet before use
Buffer	Wipe handle with surgical spirit. Wash buffing cloth in hot soapy water 60°C. Place in ultraviolet cabinet when dry
Emery board	Throw away after use
Orange stick	Throw away after use
Manicure bowl	Clean with a chemical disinfectant that will not damage the plastic surface
Spatula	Throw away after use
Workstation surface	Clean with a chemical disinfectant. Protect surfaces with clean disposable paper roll

Ellisons

TIP

Work area
The work area should be left ready for the next client whenever a treatment is completed.
Waste products should be disposed of correctly.
If you are free, help other colleagues to tidy the area after treatment to maintain the work area in readiness for the next client.

Preparation of the therapist

Make sure the treatment area is warm and comfortable and that lighting is adequate to prevent eye strain and to enable the treatment to be performed competently. Check that the area is free from obstacles that could cause a fall.

Sanitise the hands to remove surface dirt, this will also show the client you have good hygiene practice.

Preparing the work area

Check the work area to ensure that you have all the equipment, products and materials you require for the nail treatment. Use the checklist provided on page 121.

Place a clean towel over the work surface, then fold another towel into a pad and place it in the middle of the work surface. This will help support the client's forearm during treatment. Place a third towel over the pad.

The therapist will need a small towel to dry the client's hands during the treatment.

A tissue or disposable manicure mat should then be placed on top of the towels, to collect filings. This is disposed of later to avoid skin irritation from the filings.

Removing nail polish to assess the client's nail condition

Preparing the client

1 Help the client into a comfortable and relaxed position for treatment. The chair should offer adequate back and knee support, be a suitable height for the workstation and be comfortable. Ineffective positioning of the client can cause the therapist discomfort, and possibly even injury due to strain. Your elbows should be able to rest on the workstation without stretching.

2 Complete the client record card, listing all details to ensure the client's suitability for treatment.

3 If the client is wearing nail polish this must be removed to assess the client's nail condition. Use the following procedure:

a Cleanse the hands with an antiseptic applied with clean cotton wool or a spray to remove surface dirt and micro-organisms.

b Soak a clean piece of cotton wool in nail polish remover. Place over the nail plate and rest for 2–3 seconds to allow the nail polish to begin to dissolve. Apply firm strokes using the cotton wool over the nail plate surface to remove the polish. Any remaining nail polish left around the cuticle area should be removed using an orange stick tipped with cotton wool. Dip the cotton wool in nail polish remover and remove any remaining nail polish.

4 Assess the condition of the nails and skin:

a cuticles – are they dry, tight or cracked, or are they soft and supple?

b nails – are they strong, weak, brittle or flaking? Are they discoloured or stained? What shape are they – square, round, oval, long, short, bitten?

c hands – is the skin dry, rough or chapped, or is it soft and smooth?

TIP

Dark nail polish
When removing dark nail polish from the nail it might be necessary to replace the cotton wool soaked with nail polish regularly. This is because dark nail polish tends to stain the nails and surrounding skin on removal.

5 Confirm and agree with the client the treatment aim and the client's choice of nail finish.

6 Ask the client to remove jewellery from the treatment area, to prevent it becoming soiled by the massage cream/lotion. Place the jewellery in full view of the client, usually in a tissue-lined bowl.

TIP

Treatment sales opportunities
If a nail is split, a nail wrap might be completed to strengthen the nail. This should be performed by a senior therapist.

TIP

Communication is important with your client
Communication includes talking with your client (verbal communication) and also what your body language is telling the client (non-verbal communication).
You might have given a client a great basic nail treatment but will you be asked to do it again if you are not bright, cheerful and helpful?

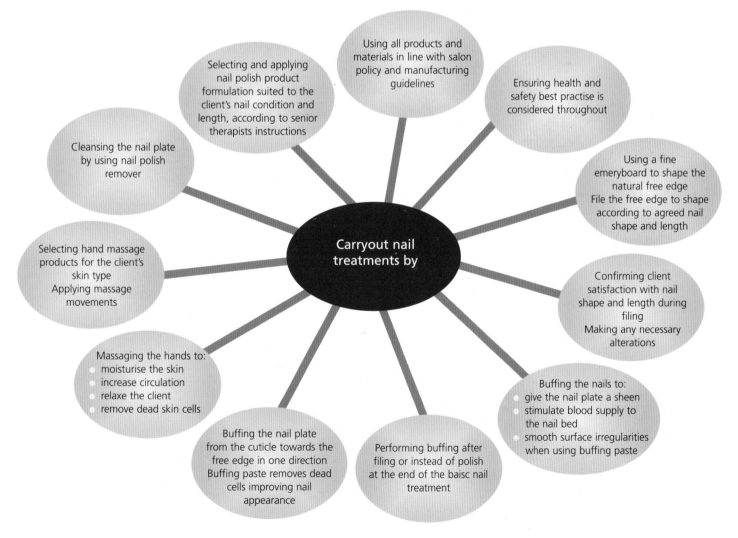

Carryout nail treatments by

Using all products and materials in line with salon policy and manufacturing guidelines

Selecting and applying nail polish product formulation suited to the client's nail condition and length, according to senior therapists instructions

Ensuring health and safety best practise is considered throughout

Cleansing the nail plate by using nail polish remover

Using a fine emeryboard to shape the natural free edge
File the free edge to shape according to agreed nail shape and length

Selecting hand massage products for the client's skin type
Applying massage movements

Confirming client satisfaction with nail shape and length during filing
Making any necessary alterations

Massaging the hands to:
- moisturise the skin
- increase circulation
- relax the client
- remove dead skin cells

Buffing the nails to:
- give the nail plate a sheen
- stimulate blood supply to the nail bed
- smooth surface irregularities when using buffing paste

Buffing the nail plate from the cuticle towards the free edge in one direction
Buffing paste removes dead cells improving nail appearance

Performing buffing after filing or instead of polish at the end of the baisc nail treatment

STEP-BY-STEP

Basic nail-treatment procedure

Briefly, the stages in a nail treatment procedure are:

1 Cleanse the client's hands with an antiseptic applied with clean cotton wool or a spray to remove surface dirt and micro-organisms. If the nails are dirty it might be necessary to soak them in warm water with a mild detergent before treatment. An orange stick tipped in cotton wool can then be used to gently clean under the free edge of the nail; care should be taken when doing this.

2 File the nails into the agreed shape and length; the part of the nail that is filed is the free edge. Use the lighter, fine textured side of the emery board when filing the nails into shape. The darker, coarser textured side of the emery board is used to remove length. File the nails from side to centre when creating an oval or round shape, with the emery board angled slightly under the free edge. To achieve a square shape, file straight across the top of the free edge in swift, strokes and gently curve the edges. File the nail length so that they are even in shape and length.

Run your finger along the edge of the free edge to ensure they are smooth, any roughness should be removed using the fine side of the emery board in an upwards stroke, this is known as bevelling.

3 Buff the nails. Buffing is used to:

    a give the nail plate a sheen

    b stimulate blood supply to increase nourishment to the nail to improve the strength and health of the nail

    c smooth surface irregularities on the nail plate, such as ridges.

Buffing is carried out after filing; it can also be used in preference to nail polish application, as in the case of a male nail treatment. If it is being used, buffing paste is applied: take a small amount from the container with a clean orange stick and apply this to each nail plate. With the fingertip, use downward strokes from the cuticle to the free edge to spread the paste over the nail plate, avoiding contact with the cuticle. Hold the buffer loosely in your hand, buff in one direction only from the cuticle towards the free edge.

Approximately six strokes are applied to each nail plate.

4 Apply hand massage after buffing. Massage is applied to:

- moisturise the skin with hand cream
- improve blood circulation and nutrition to the skin and nails
- relax the client
- remove dead skin cells and improve the appearance of the skin.

Select and apply the chosen hand cream/lotion for the client's skin type: a dry skin or male client with coarse body hair will benefit from an oil; a normal skin will benefit from a lotion. Use the following procedure:

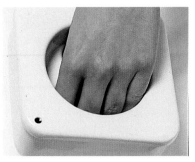

Cleansing the client's hand

Filing and shaping the nails

Buffing the nails

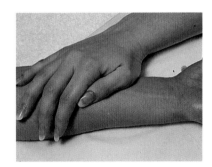

Moisturing the skin with hand cream

Massaging the hands

Massaging the fingers

Removing excess oil

Applying nail polish

TIP

Maintaining the quality of the nail polish

Clean the neck of the nail polish bottle after use to make sure that it is clean. This will ensure that the seal at the neck of the bottle is tight on closing, preventing the nail polish becoming thick.

Regularly clean the neck of the bottle with cotton wool and nail polish remover.

A product called solvent can be added to restore consistency to thick nail polish.

TIP ✔

Too much polish
Avoid having too much polish on the brush during nail polish application.
A thick application of polish will increase the time the nail polish takes to dry and could cause it to run onto the surrounding skin.

a Apply using long sweeping strokes from the client's hand to elbow, to both the inner and outer side of the forearm. Repeat 5 times.

b Using the thumbs, one in front of the other, move backwards and forwards in a sawing action from the hand to the elbow. Slide the thumbs back to the hands. Repeat twice.

c Using the same movements as in step b, using the thumbs, one in front of the other move backwards and forwards over the palm and inner forearm.

d Supporting the finger at the knuckle with one hand, hold the fingers individually and rotate the fingers clockwise and anti-clockwise. Repeat twice.

e Support the client's wrist with one hand and put your fingers between the client's fingers, grasping the hand. Circle the wrist clockwise and then anticlockwise. Repeat twice.

f Repeat step a 5 times.

5 Remove excess oil from the hand cream/lotion. Soak a cotton pad in nail polish remover. The client might find it convenient to pay for her treatment at this stage of the nail treatment to avoid damage to the nail polish after application.

6 Nail polish application: nail polish is applied to coat the nail plate for the following reasons:

- for cosmetic improvement to the nail's appearance
- to disguise stained nails
- to add strengthen weak nails
- as a specialist nail treatment, i.e. nail strengthener and ridge filler polish.

Use the following procedure:

a Remove excess grease remaining on the nail plate following the massage by applying nail polish remover to the nail plate surface with clean cotton wool. This will help the nail polish stick to the nail plate.

b Check that the edge of the nail is still smooth and even, refile as necessary.

c Select and apply nail polish according to manufacturer's instructions. The correct nail polish application techniques is shown below.

d Select a basecoat or nail strengthener polish to suit the nail condition.

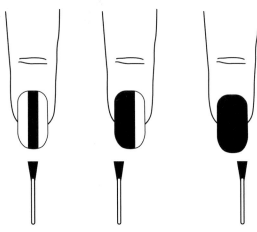

Correct polish application

TIP ✔

Fast drying spray
A fast-drying spray product can be applied to reduce the drying time of the polish

e Unscrew the bottle top to which the brush is attached. Wipe the brush on one side against the neck of the bottle, turn the brush around and apply the side of the brush with polish to the nail.

f Start with the thumb, apply three brush strokes down the length of the nail towards the cuticle, but avoid contact with the cuticle. The first stroke is down the centre of the nail and then down each side.

g Apply one coat.

h If polish comes into contact with the skin, remove with an orange stick tipped in clean cotton wool and dampened with nail polish remover.

If agreed, apply coloured polish in the same way:

a Apply two coats of a cream polish and three coats if pearlised (frosted).

b A light, neutral colour is suited to short nails. Stronger, darker colours are suited to healthy longer nails and if a dramatic effect is required.

c Apply a top coat. If using a pearlised polish, a top coat is not applied.

d Check the result meets with client and senior therapist satisfaction.

Practice your nail treatment until you can complete it in the allocated time. This is important to ensure the treatment is cost effective and clients are not delayed.

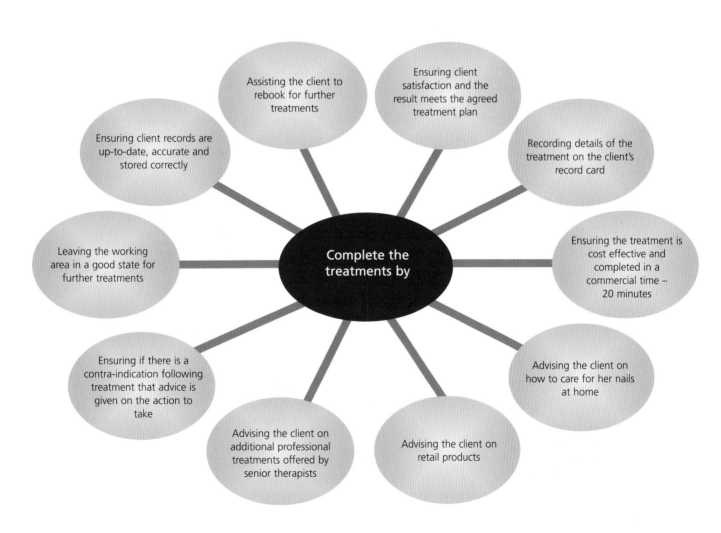

TIP

Maintaining the working area
It is important that you work in a hygienic, organized manner and that you leave the workstation neat and tidy, with all waste materials removed both during and at the end of the treatment.

Completing nail treatments

At the end of treatment, make sure the client records are up to date. This is important because you will need to refer to them in the future. The record should then be stored securely.

The client should be given home-care advice on how to care for the nails at home. This will differ for each client, depending on individual needs.

Basic home-care and advice

- Wear protective rubber gloves when washing up.
- Wear protective gloves when gardening or doing housework.
- Dry the hands thoroughly after washing.
- Apply hand cream regularly to moisturise the skin of the hands and nails.
- Avoid harsh, drying soaps.
- Do not use the fingernails as tools, this causes the nails to weaken and split and break.

Advise the client that the interval between nail treatments is usually 7–10 days.

Promoting products
Providing advice also gives you the opportunity to recommend retail products, such as nail strengthener and hand cream. This enhances the salon's retail sales and profit.

Contra-actions
Ask clients to contact the salon immediately and speak with the senior therapist if any unwanted reaction to the treatment occurs. Such *contra-actions* (e.g. an allergy, recognized by redness, swelling and inflammation) should be noted on the client's record for future reference.

TIP

Gloves
Gloves provide a barrier to protect the hands and nails from chemical detergents that could cause the skin and nails to become dry and chapped. They also prevent the nails from becoming dry causing peeling and breaking.

Glossary

Base coat	a nail-polish product applied to protect the natural nail and prevent staining from coloured nail polish
Bevelling	a nail-filing technique used at the free edge of the nail to ensure that it is smooth
Buffer	a nail tool used to improve the appearance of the nail plate and stimulate blood to the nail bed area
Buffing paste	a coarse cream with a gritty texture; it removes surface cells from the nail plate
Contra-action	an unwanted reaction to the treatment occurring during or after the treatment

Glossary

Contraindication	a reason or condition that prevents or restricts you from performing a treatment
Cuticle	the part of the skin found around the base of the nail
Data Protection Act (1998)	legislation designed to protect client privacy and confidentiality
Emery board	a nail file used to shape the free edge of the nail
Free edge	the part of the nail that grows beyond the end of the finger
Hand cream/oil	a cosmetic mixture of waxes and oils applied to soften the skin of the hands and cuticles
Massage	movements applied to the skin using the hands to improve its condition and functioning
Matrix	the growing area of the nail, found at the bottom of the nail
Nail	protective, hard shield found at the end of the fingers
Nail bed	the part of the skin covered by the nail plate
Nail plate	the part of the nail the covers the nail bed, the part of the skin upon which the nail plate rests.
Nail polish	a clear or coloured nail product that adds colour/protection to the nail
Nail strengthener	a nail-polish product that strengthens the nail plate, which has a tendency to split.
Orange stick	a disposable wooden tool for use around the cuticle and free edge of the nail
Scissors	nail tools used to shorten the length of the nail before filing
Top coat	a nail-polish product applied over another nail polish to provide additional strength and durability to the finish

Assessment and knowledge of understanding

Unit BT3: Assist with nail treatments on the hands

You have now learned how to perform a basic nail treatment to improve the appearance and condition of the hands, nails and surrounding skin. The skills developed enable you to professionally assist with nail treatments of the hands

To test your level of knowledge and understanding, answer the following short questions, these will prepare you for your summative (final) assessment.

Anatomy and physiology:

1 Draw a cross-section of the nail to show the parts:

    a matrix
    b cuticle
    c free-edge
    d nail plate
    e nail bed.

2 Briefly describe the function of each part of the nail listed above.

3 Name the four different nail shapes shown:

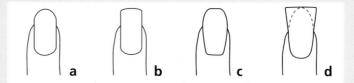

Prepare for nail treatments:

1 Name ten items required when setting up the work area for a basic nail
    treatment and explain the purpose of each.

2 Why is it important that existing nail polish is removed before treatment
    starts?

3 Why is it important that you sanitise your hands before treatments starts;
    give two reasons.

4 Why must accurate records of the client's treatment be kept?

5 Why is it important to follow the senior therapist's instructions for
    treatment application?

6 Why is it important to talk to your client during the treatment?

7 What is the purpose of the client consultation?

8 Name three contra-indications to basic nail treatment.

Assessment and knowledge of understanding

Carry out nail treatments:

1 How does buffing improve the appearance of the nails?

2 Which side of the emery board is used to reduce the length of the nails?

3 How is a square nail shape achieved when filing?

4 When would you select to use a nail strengthener?

5 State three effects of massage used in a nail treatment on the hands.

6 What is the purpose of:

   a base coat

   b top coat

7 State two effects that could be caused by incorrect technique when filing.

8 How should you position yourself when performing basic nail treatment?
   Why is your working position important?

Complete the nail treatment:

1 Why is it important to complete the nail treatment in the given time?

2 State three pieces of homecare advice that could be given to a client

3 Where should a client's records cards be stored on completion of treatment?

4 What retail product could you recommend to a client?

5 What advice would you give a client about contra-actions to treatment?

index